ASIAN DINING RULES

Essential Strategies for Eating Out at Japanese, Chinese, Southeast Asian, Korean, and Indian Restaurants

STEVEN A. SHAW

WM

WILLIAM MORROW
An Imprint of HarperCollins*Publishers*

HarperCollins book may be purchased for educational, business, or sales promotional use. For information please write: Special Markets Department, HarperCollins Publishers, 10 East 53rd Street, New York, NY 10022.

FIRST EDITION

Designed by Renato Stanisic

Library of Congress Cataloging-in-Publication Data has been applied for.

ISBN 978-0-06-125559-5

08   09   10   11   12   WBC/RRD   10   9   8   7   6   5   4   3   2   1

For my late father, Peter Shaw,
who taught me how to dine.

And for all those who came from Asia to the
New World looking for a better life.

Contents

★

Acknowledgments

★

The many restaurateurs, chefs, and other industry folks who made this book possible are not listed in these acknowledgments, but are, rather, named throughout this volume. In addition, I'd like to thank:

The many participants in the eG Forums online discussions at www.eGullet.org who offered invaluable advice, assistance, contacts, and moral support from the earliest stages of the project through its conclusion.

Those who wrote books, articles, and online resources that made my job easier. In particular: Joel Denker, author of *World on a Plate,* a superb ethnic food history (Dr. Denker also answered all my e-mails and phone calls and sent me many helpful references); Trevor Corson, author of *The Zen of Fish,* and Sasha Issenberg, author of *The Sushi Economy,* two great books on sushi; Eve Zibart, author of *The Ethnic Food Lover's Companion,* a handy reference I always kept near me while I wrote; Jeffrey Steingarten and Alex Renton for their articles, in *Vogue* and the *Guardian,* respectively, on MSG, Chinese food, and health; Lynne Olver, creator of *The Food Timeline* (www.foodtimeline.org); and all the people who have contributed Asian-food information to Wikipedia.

Author Michael Ruhlman for introducing me to Annie Chiu; Connie Nelson of the Wilmington/Cape Fear Coast Convention & Visitors Bureau for introducing me to Solange Thompson; Gita Sweeney of the Gita Group for introducing me to Ratha Chau; Karen Schloss and Frank Diaz of Diaz*Schloss Communications for introducing me to the Mehtani family; and chef Brian Bistrong for introducing me to Jenny Kwak (and Ms. Kwak for introducing me to her father, a font of wisdom on Korean-American history).

My editor, Gail Winston, her associate, Sarah Whitman-Salkin, and copyeditor, Katherine Ness, for turning my manuscript into a book. Also my previous editors at HarperCollins, Susan Friedland and Harriet Bell, for getting me this far.

My unofficial editorial team: my wife, Ellen Shapiro, my friend and colleague Dave Scantland, and my agent, Michael Psaltis, for pushing me to do my best.

Wayne and Julie Shovelin for letting me use their beach house as a writer's retreat. My mother, Penny Shaw, for all the babysitting and countless other forms of assistance. And my wife, Ellen, our son, PJ, and our bulldog, Momo, for filling our home with love.

Introduction

Empires of the Mind: My love affair with Asian food begins

In 1981, when I was twelve years old, a restaurant called Empire Szechuan Columbus opened across the street from our apartment on Manhattan's Upper West Side. It changed the course of my diet forever. This was Chinese food like I'd never before tasted: fresh, vibrant, spicy. My father, whose friend the U.S. table tennis champion (and hustler) Marty Reisman was an investor in the restaurant, and I spent years working our way through just about every dish on the exhaustive menu.

We even invented some dishes of our own, especially after my father had a heart attack and was placed on a low-fat, low-salt diet by his cardiologist and a lower-fat, lower-salt diet by my mother. In those days, low-sodium soy sauce was a niche product that you couldn't just pick up at the supermarket. My father would buy a bottle of it in Chinatown about once a year, and the Empire Szechuan kitchen would store it for use in his dishes. Lobster Cantonese was prepared for him with egg whites only, no pork. Another dish, which we named "Chicken with Red Spots," used hot chilies to liven up otherwise bland chicken with snow peas.

Outside the view of my parents, I continued to sample dishes from the less virtuous end of the spectrum. Though I'm Jewish and from New York City, I'm sure I ate more Chinese pork dumplings in the 1980s than any Chinese person—or perhaps any village—in China. I ate so many pork spare ribs that even today, pigs shudder when I approach.

What I ate the most of, however, was the Empire Szechuan egg roll, the finest specimen I'd ever tasted. Most days, on the way home from school after I got off the number 10 bus, I'd stop by and, with the carefully collected loose change in my pocket, buy an egg roll. Mary, the co-owner (and wife of the chef), who took all the orders from behind the take-out counter/hostess station, knew not to put my egg roll in a paper bag. She handed it to me, half-wrapped in a wax-paper sleeve, with a little plastic packet each of soy sauce and duck sauce. I'd bite off the top of the steaming egg roll, pour both sauces onto the exposed innards, and gleefully chomp the egg roll on my walk home. I'd have it finished by the time I crossed the street and rode the elevator up to our apartment.

If Mary was the heart of the institution, and her husband the chef its soul, the brain of Empire Szechuan Columbus was surely Mr. Chu. A former professor of mathematics from Taiwan, Mr. Chu was in charge of coordinating the restaurant's urban-planning-scale take-out and delivery operation. Mr. Chu had the preternatural ability not only to plan each deliveryman's route so as to maximize profit by minimizing time, efficiently sequencing multiple drop-offs per trip, but also to make unfailingly accurate predictions of future orders and the resources needed to accommodate them. Graph theory, the branch of mathematics used to evaluate complex networks, was Mr. Chu's specialty.

One night my father and I walked in on family meal (in the restaurant business, that's what they call the staff dinner), and Mr. Chu beckoned us over. He held up a plate of thin, curved strips of gelatinous something—maybe flesh, maybe a vegetable . . . or perhaps a dessert? It tasted like sweet, squishy bacon.

"You like?" asked Mr. Chu.

"What is it?" asked my father.

"Pig ear!" exclaimed Mr. Chu.

For the rest of my father's life, we could always get a laugh out of each other by injecting the phrase "pig ear!" (pronounced "pig eah") randomly into a conversation.

We became part of the restaurant's family. By the time I went to college, my farewell dinner was like a send-off of one of Mr. Chu's own children. He inquired after me while I was away and always had a smile and a math anecdote for me when I came home over breaks. He surely knew more about my love life than my own family, since I took every girlfriend I ever had (all two of them) to Empire Szechuan repeatedly.

At my engagement party, held in the upstairs room of the restaurant, we needed to limit the head count to the room's capacity, so we invited friends only—no parents. Mr. Chu delegated the take-out operation to Mary for the night and observed the event, all the while furiously scribbling notes in Chinese on a waiter's order pad.

Later that night, I caught my father and Mr. Chu huddled

at a table by the window. Mr. Chu had transcribed and translated into Chinese every speech given at the engagement party and was, on the fly, translating them back into English in order to relay them to my father. "And then, best man says . . ." That was also the night that Mary, for the first time in my life, came out from behind the hostess station. She was only about four and a half feet tall! All those years, unbeknownst to me, she had been sitting on a stool, making her look much taller.

Empire Szechuan is still there, though today it's called Empire Szechuan Kyoto thanks to the addition of, as is now common at Chinese restaurants, a sushi bar. Mary is still there too, as is her husband the chef, though their American-born children have no interest in the restaurant business. Mr. Chu departed long ago to open his own restaurant. My mother still lives across the street, and now my wife and I bring our two-year-old son in for dinner. They spoil him rotten. It drives my wife crazy. I don't mind.

TODAY, ONCE IN A while, I meet a fellow New Yorker who grew up on the Upper West Side, and the subject turns to Empire Szechuan. More often than not, the person I'm talking to has had a very different Empire Szechuan experience than I have. He or she sees it as an utterly unremarkable restaurant, no better or worse than a dozen others in the neighborhood and hundreds in the city.

But if you're part of a restaurant's extended family, things are different. Perhaps you've seen something like this: You walk into an Asian restaurant, and you order a few things from the menu. While you're eating your moo shoo pork, pad Thai, chicken teriyaki, or chicken tikka, you notice there's a big table of Asians across the room eating completely different food—dishes that you didn't even see on the menu.

That's because most Asian restaurants are two restaurants: the one where the outsiders eat, and the one where the insiders dine. And the good news is that you don't have to be Asian to be an insider—you just have to eat like you are. Your mission, should you choose to accept it, is to become an insider at every Asian restaurant you visit, on your first visit. This book seeks to give you the tools to do just that.

The Asian Equation: When it comes to population, sometimes quantity *is* quality

The cities in North America that have large Asian populations—Los Angeles, San Francisco, New York, Vancouver—have long had excellent Asian restaurants of all kinds. But the big story in Asian food over the past two decades has been the dramatic improvement in the quality of what's available outside those traditional bastions of Asian cuisine.

My first wake-up call on this phenomenon was in about 1998, when my wife, Ellen, and I were visiting Cave Junction, Oregon—about as small and remote a town as exists in America. We were going there to visit a winery, and the winemaker, Cliff, was giving us directions by phone. "When you drive through the town, heading in from the highway, you'll pass the diner and then two Chinese restaurants, one on each side of the road. You want to go to the one on the right, not the one on the left. It has a much better chef." I was surprised not just that Cave Junction had Chinese restaurants but also that there was a gourmet hierarchy.

Large-city dwellers still hold to the stereotype that the Asian food everywhere else in America is generic and inedible. I hear it all the time, even from people in the food press who should know better. This conventional wisdom is no more relevant today than phrenology or the theory of the flat Earth.

The quality of Asian restaurants everywhere has been improving by leaps and bounds. The supply lines have been laid in medium-size cities like Cleveland and Charlotte, such that in all their surrounding suburbs restaurants can get good ingredients—including fresh fish—from large Asian markets and suppliers that deal with Asian-operated farms in the U.S., Asian seafood distributors, and Asian spice purveyors. Most people who have been talking about these restaurants but not eating at them in the past decade would be surprised at what's out there.

At the same time, many Americans are still manifestly unadventurous when it comes to Asian food. Of the hundreds of items on a typical Chinese-restaurant menu, for example, the largest percentage of the non-Asian customers will order from a list of fifteen or so dishes, including kung pao chicken, pork fried rice, egg rolls, orange beef, sesame chicken, sweet-and-sour pork, and hot-and-sour soup. The same is true at other types of Asian restaurants. Indian restaurant owners have told me that, time and again, their non-Indian customers order mostly the same five dishes. Thai restaurants seem to sell more pad Thai than everything else put together; sushi restaurants serve up an alarming number of California rolls; and many Americans assume that Korean cuisine equals and is limited to Korean barbecue—if they've even had Korean cuisine.

I've spoken to scores of American consumers in the process of researching this book, and by far the reason cited most often for this narrow ordering pattern is lack of familiarity with the other dishes on the menu. Time and again I've heard, "I'd like to try some other dishes, but I wouldn't know where to start." This book will tell you where to start, and where to finish.

Turning the Tables: What this book is, and what it's not

A couple of years ago, I wrote an insider's guide to eating out called *Turning the Tables*. The basic mission of the book was to help readers get the most out of the restaurant experience. As opposed to restaurant reviews, which tell consumers where to eat, my project was to tell them how to dine.

One small section of the book dwelled on the matter of "Guerrilla Sushi Tactics," in other words how someone from outside the Japanese culture and lacking in sushi expertise can nonetheless get the insider's VIP experience at a sushi bar (first rule: sit at the sushi bar, not at a table in the dining room).

When I went on tour in late 2005 to promote the book, I spoke to live audiences in about ten cities and gave countless television and radio interviews. That little section on sushi elicited more inquiries and feedback than any other part of the book, and in general I was inundated with questions about ethnic restaurants, particularly Asian ones. ("Guerrilla Sushi Tactics" appears, in greatly expanded form, in Chapter I here.)

The five chapters of this book focus on five different Asian cuisine groupings: Japanese, Chinese, Southeast Asian, Korean, and Indian. (I say groupings because there are, for example, many different regional cuisines of Southeast Asia.)

This is not a cookbook. You won't find any recipes or cooking tips in these pages (unless you count the tale of my rather embarrassing first attempt at making sushi). Nor is it a book about Asia. (If you're planning a trip to Asia, what you need is a guidebook.) Rather, the goal of this book is to help you get the most out of your meals at Asian restaurants as they exist in North America today.

Each chapter begins with tales of my experiences while researching this book: time I spent in Asian restaurant kitchens, with Asian restaurant owners, at Asian markets and beyond. The purpose of these vignettes is not pedagogical but is rather to give a taste of the culture behind the cuisine. To me, enjoying food isn't just about how it tastes but also about the people, the memories, the relationships. You can learn more about sushi by befriending a sushi chef than you can from any book. I hope my tales will inspire you to reach across the cultural divide and strike up a conversation yourself.

Most of the people I spent time with are immigrants or the children of immigrants. I've found their stories inspiring, and I hope you will too. A couple of generations earlier, my own ancestors arrived on these shores to build a new life, and while they came from Europe rather than Asia, I still recognize many of the stories as variants of what my own family endured.

Because it provides a helpful context, each chapter also includes a brief history of that Asian cuisine in North America. Don't worry; I won't be taking you back through thousands of years of Asian history. Rather, these are the essential histories of Asian cultures and cuisines here in the West, and how the East and West have met to create unique new styles and flavors. By understanding the background of the food you're ordering, you may find that your experience of eating it is enriched.

Then follows a primer on the cuisine in question. I've divided each culinary primer into beginner, intermediate, and advanced sections. Regardless of your level of experience with a given cuisine, you'll find helpful information in all three sections.

The beginner material considers the needs of people who haven't had a lot of exposure to that particular cuisine. The definition of "beginner" varies a bit from cuisine to cuisine, though. For example, since most North Americans have eaten plenty of Chinese food, the beginner section of that chapter doesn't start at the level of explaining what an egg roll is. On the other hand, since many people reading this book have never been to a Korean restaurant, there I start at square one. The intermediate material assumes you're comfortable in that particular restaurant milieu, and that you're ready to branch out and try some less typical variants. The advanced section is about taking it to the next level. This is the hard-core insider stuff—the knowledge that will amaze your friends. Depending on where you live, this information may be most helpful when you travel to one of the larger cities with a significant Asian population. For example, in order to exercise your newfound knowledge of Shanghai cuisine, you'll need to be in a city with a large enough Chinese population to support a Shanghainese restaurant.

Throughout the book, I lay out the strategies for getting the most out of a restaurant: how to order the best stuff, how to conduct yourself, and other tips and tricks for crafting the most satisfying meal experience. Sometimes the advice is direct, as in explicit rules and strategies. Other times it's more subtle: I hope through the material to convey a general sense of the Asian culinary culture, which as you absorb it will make you a better-educated, more on-the-ball consumer.

Also, interspersed throughout the main narrative you'll find an eclectic collection of essays and observations, set in gray boxes, on a variety of subjects related to Asian food. It's not possible in a book of this size, or even in a five-volume set, to be comprehensive on the subject of even one Asian cuisine. At one Chinese restaurant I frequent, the annotated menu (which has lengthy descriptions of every dish, sometimes running several pages in length) is longer than this book's entire Chinese-restaurant section. So instead of pursuing the impossible goal of covering everything, I've picked and chosen my favorites. Sometimes I'll write about a subject because it's important to me (such as concerns about the treatment of Asian-restaurant workers); other times I pick a subject because I think it illustrates a point that I hope will inspire you to learn more on your own (I can't possibly write about every beverage you could drink with Asian food—that's a whole book on its own—but I hope the essay on red wine with sushi will demonstrate how much there is to explore); some of these are exercises in personal storytelling meant to illustrate the richness and diversity (and sometimes humor) of the Asian restaurant culture in North America as I've experienced it during a lifetime of eating an alarming amount of food at Asian restaurants; and still other times I just thought something was fun and interesting (as in the pieces on fortune cookies and conveyer-belt sushi).

Some chapters are longer and more detailed than others. This isn't a value judgment as to the worthiness of any given cuisine but rather a reflection of the relative availability and popularity of the different cuisines, as well as the depth of my personal experience with them. There are also, unfortunately, some cuisines that time and space couldn't accommodate. Every time I pass by the new Bhutanese restaurant in New York City, I feel a pang of guilt that I couldn't add yet another chapter here. My apologies to all the Pakistanis, Indonesians, and other representatives of the many worthy culinary cultures that I've excluded solely for reasons of space.

Though I'm based in New York City, I've traveled all over North America researching Asian restaurants, from Vancouver to Cleveland, from Winnipeg to Wilmington. You'll see profiles of restaurants in Edison, New Jersey; Washington, D.C.; New York City; and beyond. I've even dined at Asian restaurants in nine of Canada's ten provinces (sorry, Newfoundland!). This isn't a book about any one city or any specific restaurant. It's meant to apply to Asian restaurants throughout the United States and Canada (though Mexico is part of North America too, the Asian restaurant scene in Mexico is not within the purview of this book). I apologize in advance to residents of the West Coast for what may appear to be an East Coast–centric view of the world. Though I've made many trips to Vancouver (arguably the best Asian-food city in North America) and made incursions into Los Angeles and San Francisco, a few visits can never match a lifetime of experience eating in and around my hometown of New York City. I have tried mightily, however, to keep the advice in this book general, so that it will serve you equally well on either coast or anywhere in between.

While the sections of this book that explain the different cuisines can be used as a handy reference or glossary (you can certainly bring the book with you and refer to it when you dine out), this isn't a reference book. It's a book that's meant to be read. I should also warn you that because there are so many linkages and commonalities among the cuisines of Asia, information presented in one chapter often applies to another cuisine. The discussion of MSG lives in the Chinese chapter, for example, but applies to many types of Asian restaurants; if you're interested in hard data about Asian immigration and how it relates to the popularity of different types of Asian restaurants, you'll find that discussion in the Southeast Asian chapter; and the advice on "Gaming the Chinese Buffet," in the Chinese chapter, will serve you well at any kind of Asian buffet.

And while I'll offer quite a lot of advice of all kinds, it all boils down to this: I truly believe that if you love Asian restaurants, they will love you back.

TEN TIPS FOR GETTING THE MOST OUT OF EVERY ASIAN RESTAURANT MEAL

One: Become a Regular

The best restaurant isn't the one that got a good review in the local paper or a high score in the Zagat survey. It's the one where you're a regular. Being a regular affects every aspect of the dining experience, from being seated right away on a busy Saturday night, to getting the waitstaff's best service, to getting special off-menu dishes. That's especially true at family-owned restaurants, which most Asian restaurants in North America are. This news can be discouraging to some, but it needn't be to you: by being a proactive and knowledgeable customer—by taking these tips to heart—you can start getting treated like a regular on your very first visit. A special relationship with a restaurant is one of life's great pleasures, and such a relationship can be far easier and quicker to establish than many people think. You don't need to be wealthy, a celebrity, or great-looking to be a regular. (I'm none of the three, and I do pretty well in restaurants.) The benefits of being a regular will, of course, increase with each visit. Eating a first meal at a restaurant is like a first date: it's a preview that helps you decide if you're going to want a second date. Most every restaurant, like every dating partner, keeps a little something in reserve for subsequent encounters. The first meal won't expose you to the full range of an establishment's capabilities, but it will give you a taste.

Two: Do Your Homework

A family of four going out for sushi is likely to spend $150 or more on dinner. That's as much as many people spend on a digital camera or a computer printer at Costco. Yet few people take as much time to research dinner as they would to research a consumer electronics purchase. They should. A little advance work can help you choose not only the best restaurant but also the best dishes to order. Depending on where you live, there may be local guidebooks, newspaper restaurant reviews, and online resources. Pay special attention to the Internet, because traditional print media have historically not done a great job staying on top of the ethnic-restaurant scene. Online, you may very well find comments from people who've eaten their way through the whole menu at a restaurant you're considering, and sometimes you can find English translations of foreign-language menus.

Three: Go at Slow Times

The worst time to visit a restaurant is when everybody else is eating. On Saturday night during peak dinner hours, yours is just one table in a busy restaurant. But early Tuesday night you'll have the place—and all the attention—to yourself. This is a great time to meet the waitstaff and management, learn their names, and make sure they learn yours. It will be quieter too.

Four: Ask Lots of Questions

Unless you're an expert on Asian food, or you love surprises, you'll often need to ask questions in order to learn what you're ordering before you order it. Asian-restaurant menus are typically large and not particularly descriptive, so ask your server for details.

Five: Say You Want the Real Stuff

Servers in Asian restaurants have learned through experience to assume that most non-Asian customers have conservative palates. If you ask for recommendations, they'll steer you toward the menu items that are popular with Westerners. While these dishes can be delicious when done well, they're more often bland and generic. So if you want to eat outside the box, you'll have to make it clear that you want the real stuff. Don't take no for an answer.

Six: Fine-Tune Your Restaurant Radar

When you're walking or driving around and trying to pick a place to eat, look for restaurants that display individuality, not ones you recognize as chains. Also, attention to detail and clean premises demonstrate a standard of care that should carry over to the food.

Seven: Just Because It's Popular or a Bargain Doesn't Mean It's Good

If popularity were the be-all and end-all of judging restaurants, the best restaurant in the world would be McDonald's. So beware of popular surveys and full parking lots—they don't mean nearly as much as a referral from a trusted acquaintance or critic. A corollary: cheaper and bigger isn't better. A couple of dollars extra per dish can often elevate your meal far above the lowest common denominator.

Eight: Speak Up!

I know many people who were raised believing that it's poor form to complain in restaurants. But a restaurant meal isn't dinner at a friend's home—it's something you pay for with your hard-earned money. So if you're not satisfied with your experience, speak up. Be polite but firm, and most of the time, you'll get what you want (the rest of the time you'll at least know you did what you could). When complaining, however, tell it to someone who can do something about it. Your server usually has little power to fix a situation, and of course complaining the next day or week won't solve anything. Instead, as soon as you see a problem, excuse yourself from the table (as if you're going to the washroom, which also saves you the discomfort of complaining in front of your guests) and find a manager. There's a flip side to complaining, though: you should also offer praise when things go well.

Nine: Don't Sweat the Language Barrier

Unless you grew up in Asia, you're probably not going to be able to pronounce the names of Asian-restaurant dishes all that well. Even people from one part of China can barely pronounce the dishes from other parts of China. So don't worry about it. Smile, speak up, and do the best you can. Nobody is going to hold it against you. They may even find it charming.

Ten: Keep an Open Mind and Take Some Risks

If you order the same five familiar dishes every time you go out for Asian food, you'll always be safe but you'll never discover that sixth dish that you like even better. Try something new each time you go out to eat, and don't be disappointed if you get the occasional dud. It's like dating: you need to meet a lot of people before you find the one you love. Except with food you don't have to be monogamous: you can love as many dishes as you want and the others won't complain.

CHAPTER I

Japanese

Sushi Is My Wife: A history with swords and half-bird men

Morimoto, Nobu, Masa: in the culture of sushi, it's common to name a restaurant after its owner. Hideo Kuribara's tiny restaurant in Manhattan's SoHo, however, is named Ushiwaka Maru.

According to samurai legend, Ushiwaka Maru was trained in swordcraft by the Tengu, a clan of mythological half-human/half-bird creatures known for their skills in the martial arts. Slight of build, Ushiwaka Maru made up for his diminutive stature with preternatural swiftness and dexterity. It is said that his sword technique was so deft that he could slice the falling leaves of trees in half. He also played the flute.

The twelfth-century warrior-monk Benkei had taken possession of the Goyo bridge in Kyoto, defeating every sword-bearer who attempted to cross. A giant, Benkei had disarmed 999 opponents, keeping their swords as trophies. Ushiwaka Maru set out to face him.

Playing his flute as he strolled, Ushiwaka Maru came upon Benkei at the bridge. In the ensuing clash, skill proved mightier than strength, and Benkei never got that 1,000th sword. Instead, after being disarmed by Ushiwaka Maru, Benkei swore eternal allegiance to him. With his vassal at his side, Ushiwaka Maru (then going by Minamoto Yoshitsune, his adult samurai name, bestowed at his coming-of-age ceremony) achieved decisive victory in the Genpei wars.

"Ushiwaka Maru is my soul mate," announces sushi chef Hideo Kuribara as he pulls open his traditional summer kimono to reveal a tee-shirt painted with a scene of Ushiwaka Maru defeating Benkei at the bridge. It's late: nearly 2 A.M. My friend Raji and I have been sitting at the sushi bar for hours after the restaurant's close as Hideo regales us with stories and opinions, slipping from English to Japanese and back without warning. Good thing Raji is here to translate.

"Ushiwaka Maru is my inspiration." Perhaps, but Hideo looks to be more in Benkei's weight class than Ushiwaka Maru's. In addition to having Ushiwaka Maru's skills with a blade (albeit a sushi knife rather than a sword), Hideo is built like a football player, has the shaved head of a warrior-monk, and holds black belts in both karate and judo ("I never have a problem in my restaurant").

Born in 1961 in the Tokyo suburb of Gunma, Hideo received his sushi training from then-eighty-year-old master Sadao Maneyama, the author of an authoritative sushi text and the owner of the sushi restaurant chain Kintaro. While it's possible to take courses in the United States and become a "certified" sushi chef in a matter of weeks, traditional Japanese sushi apprenticeships last for years. Hideo spent his first four years of apprenticeship cutting intricate decorative bamboo leaves for sushi platters, never once making a piece of sushi. After passing a series of timed leaf-cutting tests, Hideo progressed to a year of making only the sushi rolls called maki before being allowed to make individual pieces of nigiri sushi.

Hideo moved on to the restaurant company Sushidokoro Taguchi, where he rose quickly through the ranks. But after visits to Hawaii and Los Angeles, where he was disappointed with the available sushi offerings, Hideo became obsessed with the holy grail of bringing traditional sushi to America: he dreamed of opening his own restaurant in New York City. So he took a job with the Sushiden company, which operates sushi restaurants in Japan and had also just opened a restaurant in midtown Manhattan. Though lured to Sushiden by the prospect of being stationed in New York, Hideo was never actually offered a transfer (upon reflection, he notes, he never asked). Eventually he accepted an offer from another restaurant, Chinzan-So, which was in the Four Seasons Hotel Tokyo and, Hideo had heard, had plans to open a branch in New York.

The transfer came through and Hideo was off to JFK airport. Much to his surprise, however, New York Chinzan-So was not in New York but in New Jersey, in a shopping center on the Hudson River overlooking Manhattan. With his limited English and general lack of worldliness (due to spending most of his adult life with fish, rice, and bamboo leaves), it took Hideo a while to figure out he wasn't even in New York. He slowly saved enough to open his own restaurant, but he couldn't afford New York real estate prices, so he stayed in New Jersey, where he had the dubious distinction of running the best sushi restaurant in the history of Cliffside Park. In 2003, nine years and seven months after arriving in America, Hideo finally opened his dream restaurant, Ushiwaka Maru, in Manhattan.

BACK IN THE TWELFTH century, fortune turned against Ushiwaka Maru when his unscrupulous brother, Yoritomo, betrayed him. Ushiwaka Maru and Benkei spent two years on the run, avoiding detection through guile and trickery, but at the end they—along with Ushiwaka Maru's family and remaining followers—were surrounded in the castle of Takadachi. Capture appeared inevitable. Ushiwaka Maru first killed his family so they wouldn't fall into enemy hands. Then he committed *seppuku*—Japanese ritual suicide.

Benkei blocked the doorway to Ushiwaka Maru's chambers. The enemy shot him full of arrows. Benkei took so many long arrows to his body that when he died, he remained propped upright by their shafts. So great had his bravery been that out of respect none of the enemy soldiers would step past Benkei's body.

MOST MODERN-DAY SUSHI COUNTERS follow a single design scheme, with a glass display case standing between the chef's work space and the customers' eating area. Hideo never liked that arrangement, because the glass case blocks the customer's view of the chef's hands. For the restaurant Ushiwaka Maru, Hideo worked with his contractor to engineer a custom sushi bar that keeps the food preparation in full view: the chefs' work area is elevated and the cutting surfaces are at the customers' eye level. The sushi display cases cascade down and toward the customers, who eat from a counter approximately a foot below. When the chefs need fish, they tilt the display case doors toward the customers and reach in from above. The customer sees every cut, every move, every specimen of fish (this top-access design is also the most efficient from a refrigeration standpoint). At Ushiwaka Maru, there's nowhere to hide. And there's nothing *to* hide: Ushiwaka Maru serves some of the highest quality sushi available outside Japan.

Needless to say, in order to operate in full view, Hideo and his two assistant sushi chefs must maintain a degree of cleanliness and organization that is exceptional even by the already high hygienic standards of traditional Japanese sushi bars. The chefs at Ushiwaka Maru are constantly cleaning the counter, their hands, and their knives, so that the sushi preparation area has the spotlessness of a secret research facility or hospital operating room of the future. Nonetheless, Hideo has been repeatedly sanctioned by New York's Department of Health for failure to wear latex gloves when making sushi. No amount of hand washing, no amount of time wasted in administrative hearings explaining that sushi is traditionally made with the hands, no amount of pleading that bare hands are necessary to judge the quality and safety of raw fish, has prevented Hideo from being penalized (the restaurant was recently shuttered for several months while Hideo installed all new refrigeration in order to comply with health codes). As the Department of Health puts it, "Food worker does not use proper utensil to eliminate bare hand contact with food that will not receive adequate additional heat treatment." Hideo is in the process of asking the Japanese government to intervene.

During the U.S. occupation of Japan after World War II, samurai swords and martial arts were outlawed, and sword makers found themselves with no market. They turned instead to making kitchen knives, and today Japanese cutlery is considered by many chefs to be the world's finest. Hideo's main sushi knife, called a *deba,* was handmade by the descendants of samurai sword makers and cost $3,000.

Between buying fish (much of his fish comes from Japan, and he spends hours on the phone with his suppliers each week), processing the fish (every kind of fish requires special, expert handling in order to break it down into the rectangular blocks needed for the dinner service), running his restaurant (which serves until midnight six days a week), practicing martial arts (luckily there's a judo studio right across Houston Street), and arguing the case for traditional sushi preparation methods (unsuccessfully, so far), Hideo has time for little else. He doesn't go out much, and he doesn't have a lot of friends. "I never marry," Hideo says with a shrug while sharpening his deba at 2 A.M. "Sushi is my wife."

SUSHI: MYTH AND REALITY

MYTH: *Sushi* means "raw fish."

REALITY: The word *sushi* in Japanese actually refers to rice. Specifically, rice seasoned with vinegar. While much sushi does include raw fish, it can also include cooked fish or even nonfish ingredients. If it doesn't contain rice, however, it's not sushi. Pieces of raw fish without rice are referred to as *sashimi*.

MYTH: You eat sushi with chopsticks.

REALITY: There's no need to struggle with chopsticks. It's entirely acceptable etiquette in Japan to pick up sushi with your (washed) hands. Go ahead. It's okay. If you do choose to use chopsticks, however, here's a good trick: tip each piece of sushi on its side before picking it up. That way, the chopsticks will be pinching the fish against the rice, ensuring that the piece won't fall apart.

MYTH: Sushi is made using just-caught fish.

REALITY: Most fish used in making sushi has been frozen at some point, either on the boat, at a processing facility, or even in the restaurant. (In the United States, FDA guidelines require this, though not all states enforce those guidelines as vigorously as they could.) Moreover, not all fish is best when just caught. Some is intentionally aged to develop flavor and character, just like the best beef—albeit for days, not weeks.

MYTH: That stuff in the California roll is crab.

REALITY: The stuff in the California roll contains no crab at all. It's a manufactured product called *surimi* and is often sold retail as "crab stick" or "sea legs." The meat of various white-fleshed fish like hake and tilapia is pulverized and mixed with additives to create a shellfish-like texture and flavor. Because surimi contains no shellfish, it's even available in a kosher-certified version.

MYTH: That green stuff is wasabi.

REALITY: You've probably never tasted real, fresh, pure wasabi. Wasabi is a root related to but not the same as horseradish. Very few Japanese restaurants, even in Japan, use real wasabi, which pound for pound is more expensive than bluefin tuna. Rather, they use a reconstituted powdered product made from regular horseradish and green food coloring, and perhaps in the more expensive products a tiny percentage of powder made from real wasabi. Everybody refers to this green stuff as wasabi (for the sake of comprehensibility, I do it too in this book), but it isn't. Only at the very best Japanese restaurants—and then often only by request—can you get fresh wasabi, which must be grated to order (usually with a sharkskin grater) because it deteriorates so quickly, and it is mostly white with just a hint of green.

MYTH: You mix the wasabi with the soy sauce and dip the sushi in it.

REALITY: Not if you want to taste the sushi. A well-made piece of sushi is already a complete little package. There's even a little bit of wasabi in it. Dipping your sushi in soy sauce and wasabi (or, worse, eating a piece of pickled ginger with it) without tasting it is the equivalent of pouring salt and ketchup on your food without tasting it. At most, well-made sushi should require a small bit of soy sauce (turn the pieces upside-down and dip the fish, not the rice, in the soy sauce) and, if you like extra heat, a faint smear of wasabi.

MYTH: Rolls aren't real sushi.

REALITY: Rolls, or *maki*, absolutely are real sushi. Sushi purists don't object to all rolls, only to the junked-up Westernized rolls that contain ingredients like cream cheese. But if you go to the best sushi restaurants anywhere in the world, you'll certainly see maki on the menu.

MYTH: Sushi is really hard to make.

REALITY: It may be incredibly hard to make sushi at a world-class level, but with a little practice you can make better sushi at home than you can buy at the supermarket. Rolls, especially, are easy to make once you get the hang of it. Many Asian markets, and even some Western supermarkets, sell kits to get you started. Your guests will be amazed.

MYTH: Eating sushi is risky.

REALITY: Any food is dangerous if improperly handled, but sushi is no more dangerous than anything else. Indeed, Japanese restaurants tend to be fanatical about cleanliness.

Sushi Rising: West meets East, West falls in love with East

Although sushi has taken center stage as the iconic Japanese food in the minds of most Westerners, and is now available in the refrigerator cases of local supermarkets throughout North America, it is a relatively recent arrival on these shores, dating to the 1960s. Most people in North America over the age of thirty-five had sushi-free childhoods, and outside the major coastal cities there was little sushi to speak of prior to the 1980s.

Not surprisingly, the sushi phenomenon established its North American beachhead in California, which has always had not only the largest Japanese population but also the most convenient air-travel and cargo routes to Japan. Prior to the 1960s, however, Japanese food in North America meant sukiyaki, tempura, and teriyaki.

The first Japanese immigrants came to California around 1869; the United States Census of 1870 counted just fifty-five Japanese in the United States. Fifteen years later, in 1884, Hamanosuke Shigeta opened the first recorded Japanese restaurant in California, called Charlie Hama's Restaurant, at 340 East 1st Street in Los Angeles, marking the birth of that city's Little Tokyo.

The dual events of Japanese internment during World War II, which disrupted most Japanese-owned businesses, and the Los Angeles city plan of 1950, which uprooted many Little Tokyo eating and drinking establishments in order to make way for the new headquarters of the Los Angeles Police Department, left the California Japanese restaurant business in shambles. But it rebuilt quickly. The restaurant Kawafuku, one of the few to survive the real estate shake-up, became popular with Hollywood stars (who have historically been food-trend trailblazers), as did new Japanese restaurants like Eigiku, established in 1954.

In the 1960s, the radical increase in Japanese businesspeople stationed in California led the owner of Kawafuku, Nakajima Tokijiro, to install a sushi bar on the restaurant's second floor. Immediately popular with Japanese people, it also became popular with some Westerners whom the Japanese businessmen brought as guests. Eigiku opened its own sushi bar in 1962 with chef Koya Eiichi at the helm, and soon after that, Eiichi opened Tokyo Kaikan, which eventually had its own sushi bar under chef Mashita Ichiro.

Sushi spread quickly up the West Coast and to the largest North American cities, and by 1967 Shiro's had opened in Seattle and Kiro had opened in Chicago (both are still in operation). In New York, a restaurant called the Nippon was serving sushi as of 1963, and New York had its own sushi boom in the 1970s. Today the center of gravity for cutting-edge sushi has arguably shifted to New York (most notably, the renowned chef Masa Takayama relocated his restaurant from Los Angeles to New York in 2004). It took longer for sushi to penetrate the interior: the restaurant Koto in Tennessee displays a sign: THE OLDEST SUSHI BAR IN NASHVILLE. ESTABLISHED, 1985.

The array of fish available at even an average North American sushi bar today—reliable, well-handled, diverse—did not exist in the 1960s and '70s. There were no international airshipping routes for fish: the first bluefin tuna weren't flown across the Pacific until 1972, and superfreezing technology developed much later. (True World Foods, a venture of Reverend Sun Myung Moon's Unification Church, aka "the Moonies," has been a major force in the development of the sushi-fish distribution system, and many of North America's best sushi restaurants are customers.) Early sushi restaurants in North America had to make do with limited, seasonally volatile selections of locally caught fish. Bluefin tuna, which had become central to the sushi culture in Japan, was rarely available in California, and as a result the California roll was born.

Chef Mashita Ichiro of Tokyo Kaikan is widely credited with the invention of the California roll, the original intent of which was to substitute the lusciousness of avocado for the texture of bluefin tuna. The California roll also sought to appeal to American palates: it is formed inside-out, with the nori (seaweed) wrapper on the inside and the rice on the outside (traditional maki are made the other way around, with the nori on the outside), so as not to seem too strange to Westerners, and it contains no raw fish (only cooked crab or surimi). Over time, inventive sushi chefs in the West developed a whole culture of inside-out rolls, and today there are hundreds of original creations named for everything from cities to celebrities to mythical beasts, utilizing ingredients from smoked salmon and cream cheese to peanut butter and jelly.

Japanese food culture has also been influential in American cuisine, particularly at the fine-dining level. In the 1990s in particular, Asian ingredients—especially Japanese ones—started to appear everywhere in contemporary American restaurants. The minimalism of French nouvelle cuisine, too, is thought by many to have been influenced by Japanese cuisine and aesthetics.

At the same time, Western food culture has had a substantial impact on Japan. Tempura—indeed the entire phenomenon of deep frying—was introduced to Japan by the Portuguese. The taste for beef, forbidden by law in Japan from the sixteenth through the nineteenth centuries, developed thanks to trade with the West. That meat-oriented palate was responsible for the rise in popularity of the bluefin tuna, which a century ago was not a significant sushi fish. The American occupation of Japan triggered the opening of many sushi bars because the regulations and rationing system under General MacArthur allowed sushi restaurants to thrive (Japanese were allowed to use their rice rations to buy sushi).

The West continues to influence Japan today, not only in the sense of McDonald's but also in influencing Japanese cuisine itself. America's most famous sushi chef, Nobu Matsuhisa, recently opened a branch of his Nobu restaurant (co-owned by Robert De Niro) in Tokyo. Inside-out rolls in the style of the California roll have been gaining popularity in Japan. Traditional Japanese cuisine, which evolved slowly in Japan, developed much more rapidly in the West, where inventiveness was unleashed without the restrictions of tradition.

According to the report "Japanese Restaurants Outside Japan," published by the Ministry of Agriculture, Forestry, and Fisheries of Japan, there are now approximately 10,000 Japanese restaurants in North America, a 250 percent increase over the past decade (the current rate of growth is 8.5 percent per year). That number doesn't include countless supermarkets and other food-service operations that sell sushi and other Japanese foods. Fewer than 10 percent of Japanese restaurants in North America are Japanese-owned, however. Most are owned and managed by Asian immigrants of Chinese, Korean, and Vietnamese extraction.

BELT TIGHTENING

When my wife, Ellen, and I were on our honeymoon in Vancouver, on our first night in town we took a stroll down Robson Street, Vancouver's main drag. We encountered a sign out front of a staircase leading up to a restaurant named Tsunami Sushi. The sign mysteriously read VANCOUVER'S ONLY FLOATING SUSHI BAR. What could it mean? We entered and were shown to seats at a counter, and when the dining room came into focus we found ourselves staring at the most unusual regatta: Before us, behind and slightly above the counter, was a canal filled with water. This canal circled the entire restaurant, flowing past every seat at the wrap-around counter. In the canal were flat wooden boats, connected to one another with little chains—boat after boat after boat. The boats were sailing methodically around the restaurant, as in a child's fantasy. And on the flat deck of each boat was a rectangular plate of sushi.

The little instruction card on the table said to take whatever we wanted from the boats. There were several different designs of plates, each of which corresponded to a different price. At the end of the meal, the plates would be collected and tabulated, and a bill presented.

It's not that the sushi was all that great. It was average. But the spectacle, the convenience, the value . . . we went back almost every day for a week.

The restaurant we stumbled across in Vancouver was what in Japan is called a *kaiten sushi* (literally "rotating sushi") restaurant. In English it's most often referred to as "conveyer-belt sushi," and indeed conveyer belts are more common and traditional than canals.

Conveyer-belt sushi dates back to 1958, when a restaurateur in Japan named Yoshiaki Shiraishi couldn't find enough staff for his popular sushi restaurant. The story runs that, as Yoshiaki Shiraishi was taking a brewery tour, he watched the conveyer belts and put two and two together: why not use conveyer belts instead of waiters? He adapted the technology and determined the optimal speed so that the sushi would be easy for customers to pick up but not so slow as to take forever to circumnavigate the restaurant. That speed, by the way, is exactly eight centimeters per second.

Today there are nearly 3,000 kaiten sushi restaurants in Japan, and kaiten sushi is a $2 billion business. At the height of his success, Yoshiaki Shiraishi operated 240 restaurants under the brand name Mawaru Genroku Sushi. While there have been examples of kaiten sushi restaurants outside Japan for several decades, there was an export boom in the 1990s when Japan's economy went through a contraction, thus forcing kaiten equipment manufacturers to look overseas for new business.

The basic technology of kaiten sushi has remained unchanged since 1958, but there have been some innovations. Counters are not conducive to large groups of diners, so over time kaiten sushi restaurants started adding tables perpendicular to the conveyer belt, so larger groups could sit face to face (the two people at the end of the table get the sushi for everyone else). Radio-frequency identification (RFID) microchips have been embedded in the plates in order to track inventory; if a plate stays on the conveyer beyond a certain length of time, a scanner detects it and the kitchen is instructed to remove it. Some restaurants have experimented with automatic plate-counting machines.

And it is now common for kaiten sushi restaurants to have touch-screen ordering terminals at the tables that allow customers to put in special requests. These are produced by the kitchen and sent out on the conveyer belt with special flags to mark that they're going to a certain table. This technology has not only reduced waste from 7 percent to 2 percent at many restaurants but has also attracted new customers: some restaurants report a 30 percent increase in customers after installing the system.

Moreover, some larger-scale kaiten sushi operations now use machines to make the sushi, at least in part: the rice balls for nigiri pieces are often formed by machines referred to as "sushi robots." It seems inevitable that, someday, basic food preparation and service tasks will be performed by machines. At the luxury end of the dining spectrum, where culinary artistry is emphasized, there may always be a need for the human element. But for basic sustenance, technology may very well make participation by humans unnecessary. So if you have a chance to check out a conveyer-belt sushi restaurant, you should. It's a glimpse of the future.

In Japan, women and families in particular gravitate toward kaiten sushi because the experience is less intimidating than that of the traditional sushi bar, which can be the domain of well-to-do businessmen and their dates.

Kaiten sushi is rarely great, but those who love sushi love it at many levels, just as true hamburger lovers may enjoy the occasional fast-food burger even though they realize the burger at the best steakhouse in town is much better (and much more expensive).

Understanding Sushi

BEGINNER: BASIC SUSHI

Most sushi falls into one of two categories: *maki sushi* or *nigiri sushi*. Maki are the rolls; nigiri are the individual pieces.

Maki Sushi

If you're just getting into sushi, maki sushi (meaning "rolled sushi") is a great place to start. The basic maki offerings at any Japanese restaurant (or other Asian restaurant that serves sushi, or even your local supermarket) tend not to be strongly flavored—they're not "too fishy."

Maki sushi comes in many forms, the most common being *hoso-maki* and *ura-maki*. The long, thin rolls, about an inch in circumference, are usually cut up into six or eight small cylindrical pieces.

In hoso-maki, the main ingredient, for example tuna (*tekka*), is in the middle, surrounded by rice, a little wasabi, and, on the outside, a nori wrapper. When the papery seaweed wrapper comes in contact with the moist rice, the flavors activate and the nori becomes a delicious edible container for the maki (however, after too much time, it just becomes soggy). Hoso-maki made with tekka would be called tekka-maki (tuna roll); hoso-maki made with cucumber (*kappa,* named for a mythical Japanese creature who loves cucumbers) are kappa-maki. There are quite a few vegetarian maki options available, such as avocado, asparagus, yamaimo (crunchy mountain yam), umeboshi (pickled plum), oshinko (pickled daikon radish), and kampyo (pickled gourd).

Ura-maki are similar to hoso-maki but are constructed inside-out. The fish or other filling is in the center of the roll, wrapped in nori, and on the outside is a layer of rice, usually garnished with sesame seeds or fish roe. Ura-maki are wildly popular in North America and many other places outside Japan, where they've become the blank canvas for the creativity of many sushi chefs. The most familiar example of ura-maki is the California roll, with its filling of avocado, imitation crabmeat, fish roe, and mayonnaise.

The traditionalist sushi chefs back in Japan used to scoff at ura-maki. However, these creative rolls have captured the public imagination around the world, and many chefs in Japan have responded to the demand by embracing the style and creating inside-out rolls of their own. Today you can even get California rolls in Japan.

There are no limits to the creative possibilities with sushi rolls. I've seen everything from rolls made with red meat, to rolls made with cheese, to dessert rolls made with sweet rice and fruit fillings. The maki format lends itself to experimentation.

You probably won't find that you need to use the terms hoso-maki and ura-maki in any actual dining contexts, though. For the most part any given roll defaults to one or the other format. You can, however, ask for a roll that's normally made as hoso-maki to be made "inside-out" if you prefer it that way.

Besides the California roll, the following are some of the more common ura-maki. You may find minor variants at your local sushi bar, or you may find these same rolls going by another name (such as a name derived from the restaurant or town where you're dining), but these are the standard definitions.

Caterpillar roll: avocado, eel, and "antennae" fashioned out of julienned carrot

Dynamite roll: deep-fried battered shrimp (tempura), avocado, cucumber, and mayonnaise

Spider roll: fried soft-shell crab, cucumber, avocado, lettuce, and spicy mayonnaise

Philadelphia roll: smoked salmon, cream cheese, cucumber, and scallion

BC roll (as in British Columbia, Canada): grilled salmon skin, cucumber, and a sweet sauce

Godzilla roll: deep-fried battered yellowtail (*tempura hamachih*), teriyaki and hot sauces, and scallion

Nigiri Sushi

When making nigiri sushi, the sushi chef forms an oblong of rice with his palms, smears it with a hint of wasabi, then lays a slice (*neta*) of raw fish (or another ingredient, like broiled eel) on top. Occasionally, either for decoration or to hold it together, nigiri sushi is circumscribed by a thin band of nori.

The following are the nigiri toppings you are most likely to meet at sushi bars in North America.

Anago: conger eel broiled and brushed with a sweet sauce

Ebi: shrimp

Hirame: flounder

Ika: squid

Ikura: salmon roe

Kani: crab

Maguro: tuna

Otoro: fatty tuna

Saba: mackerel

Sake: salmon

Tako: octopus

Unagi: eel

Uni: sea urchin roe

In addition to fish, egg is a common nigiri sushi topping, in the form of a slightly sweetened, layered omelette called *tamago yaki,* or just *tamago* for short. The care with which a sushi chef makes tamago is often a good indicator of the attention to detail paid to the rest of the sushi.

Sashimi

Most any fish that can be ordered as nigiri sushi can also be eaten as sashimi. *Sashimi* means thin slices or small pieces of fish, without the rice and without anything else. It's the purest, most delicate experience of the fish, and if you order sashimi you should eat it before moving on to sushi. Ordering tuna sashimi is often an excellent litmus test for the quality of a sushi bar.

INTERMEDIATE: BEYOND THE BASIC SUSHI TYPES

Once you've got a handle on the basic maki and nigiri sushi options, there are a few additional formats of sushi you may enjoy experimenting with. If you try to look up these terms online or in books, remember that sushi can sometimes be spelled "zushi," especially when combined with another word. Also, the hyphens are optional. I use them for clarity, but where I write "oshi-sushi" someone else could easily write "oshizushi."

Gunkan-maki, or warship roll. Gunkan-maki was invented in Japan in the 1930s (at a restaurant called Ginza Kubei) as a way of making sushi with soft, slippery, and runny ingredients like salmon roe, oysters, urchin, and quail eggs, which would get squeezed out of a normal maki or slip off a normal piece of nigiri. In gunkan-maki, the sushi chef forms an oval of rice and then builds a collar around it with a sheet of nori that extends above the level of the rice, forming a vessel for the soft topping. It's best eaten in one bite.

Futo-maki, or fat roll. Futo-maki are just like regular maki, except they're quite a bit larger in diameter—easily an inch and a half to two inches. Futo-maki normally contain several ingredients—mostly vegetables—and are designed in part to enhance their kaleidoscopic appearance. (I've heard some sushi chefs refer to futo-maki, off the record, as "the BFR," short for "big f——ing roll.")

Te-maki, or hand roll. Here, a sheet of nori is formed into a cone, usually about four inches long, and filled with the rice and toppings.

Inari-sushi, or stuffed sushi. Named after the Shinto god Inari, who was said to love fried tofu, Inari-sushi has no fish or any other garnish. It's just a pouch of fried tofu filled with rice. I wouldn't want to make an entire meal of inari-sushi, but its subtle flavors are enjoyable when it's part of a larger progression of foods. Kids love it.

Oshi-sushi, or pressed sushi. This isn't very common in North America, but some restaurants offer it, and it's worth seeking out for its unusual, beautiful appearance and denser-than-regular-sushi texture. Using a rectangular wooden mold called an *oshibako*, the sushi chef lays the fish or other toppings on the bottom. Then he adds a layer of rice, fits a lid into the mold, and presses down to create a block. The block is unmolded by inverting the oshibako, so the toppings are on top and the rice on the bottom. Then the block is cut into little squares and served.

Chirashi-sushi, or scattered sushi. A popular lunchtime dish, this is certainly the easiest kind of sushi to make at home because it requires no particular rolling or shaping skills. It's a bowl of sushi rice with the other ingredients scattered throughout.

BEYOND TRYING NEW TYPES of sushi on your own, the best way to advance your knowledge is to let a sushi chef guide you. Most every sushi restaurant offers a variety of chef's specials, from a basic sushi platter, to a deluxe sushi platter, to a deluxe platter containing both sashimi and sushi. These platters offer a great deal: in exchange for you giving over the decision-making rights to the chef, the chef gives you a balanced selection of sushi. And if you're flexible enough to order this way, you can save some serious money. I priced out several sushi platters at their per-piece rates, and you can easily achieve a 50-percent savings. For example, at one restaurant in New York, a sushi platter consisting of ten pieces of nigiri sushi and one maki roll costs $21. The individual pieces of nigiri, if ordered separately, would be $3.25 a piece, plus $5.25 for the maki, for a total of $37.75. That's a savings of $16.75.

A sushi platter will introduce you to some new types of

fish and will demonstrate a balanced approach to composing a sushi meal. The ultimate sushi experience, however, is *omakase*. When you tell a sushi chef at any of the better sushi restaurants, "*Omakase*," you're asking the chef to design a customized tasting menu for you. *Omakase* (pronounced "oh-ma-ka-say") literally means "entrust." You agree on a price, usually a high price (omakase is *not* a way to save money), or if you're brave you can leave the price open-ended, and the chef chooses the very best of what's available at the restaurant and serves it piece by piece over the course of your meal. If you order omakase at the sushi bar and your chef is communicative, it's also a great way to get some sushi lessons.

ADVANCED: FRESH TO FERMENTED

Every sushi bar offers tuna (*maguro*), and most offer two varieties: *akami* and *toro*. Akami is regular red tuna, and toro is cut from the tuna's belly, where the flesh is extra-fatty.

But that's only the beginning. At the very best sushi restaurants, you can get a dizzying variety of tuna cuts. A tuna is a huge fish, and the meat from different parts of the body is noticeably different. Top sushi restaurants make several distinctions based on the part of the tuna the meat comes from. At Sushi Yasuda in New York City, there are usually five (and sometimes more) variants of tuna on offer.

The main subdivisions of toro are *o-toro* and *chu-toro*. The o-toro is the fattiest, and the chu-toro is somewhere between regular tuna and toro. O-toro is more prized than chu-toro, but I actually like chu-toro better because o-toro can be overwhelmingly fatty. Furthermore, o-toro is divided into two subcategories: *shimofuri* and *dandara*.

Shimofuri means "falling frost" and refers to the pieces of o-toro that have even flecks of fat throughout. Dandara has the fat running through it in a striped pattern.

Yellowtail (the Japanese amberjack, not to be confused with yellowfin tuna) is another fish where there are multiple subdivisions. Most people who eat sushi think yellowtail is synonymous with the term *hamachi*, and indeed at most sushi restaurants hamachi is the only type of yellowtail available. At Sushi Yasuda and other top sushi restaurants, however, there can be as many as four on offer. Unlike tuna, where the distinctions are largely based on location within the fish's anatomy, the differences among yellowtail varieties have to do with the age of the fish. For this reason, it is called an "ascending fish." The youngest yellowtail, less than fifteen centimeters long, is called *wakashi*. At forty centimeters it's called *inada* or *hamachi*. At sixty centimeters it's called *warasa*, and at seventy centimeters it's called *buri*. (These designations vary by region in Japan, but if you know any of them you're way ahead of even most Japanese people.) Tasting the four varieties side by side is similar to tasting lamb at different ages, from baby lamb to mutton.

There's one type of sushi that can only be considered very advanced: *nare-sushi*, meaning "matured sushi," is the original sushi, and it's hard-core. Nare-sushi is an acquired taste, and most Japanese people don't even bother to acquire it. The preparation involves lengthy fermentation in barrels. First, the fish is skinned, gutted, salted, and weighted down under a stone (the stone is called a *tsukemonoishi*). After a few days, the fish is soaked and then layered in another barrel, this time in alternating layers of rice and fish. Six months later, a stinky-cheese-like fermented fish product emerges. If you can find it, try it. Once.

Comparing nare-sushi to the sushi of today makes for an interesting contrast: sushi started out as a way to preserve fish, yet today it's all about the freshest possible fish. Along the way, thanks to improvements in refrigeration and transportation, the entire raison d'être of sushi reversed itself.

MAKING SUSHI AT HOME, WITHOUT A CLUE

Sushi has been the butt of Western jokes for decades. Every time I tell someone I'm writing about sushi, I hear "The Japanese are so impatient they can't even wait to cook their fish!" or "How can they call someone a sushi chef when he doesn't cook anything!" Patience and culinary skill, however, are hallmarks of any good sushi chef, as I was reminded when I set out one day to make sushi at home.

I didn't wake up and decide to make sushi. Rather, I was inspired by a trip to the supermarket. On the shelf, in between the white and brown Texmati rices, there was a "Sushi Rice" offering. It got me thinking. I eat a lot of sushi, I opine about sushi in various outlets, I'm writing a book with a substantial section on sushi, yet I've never tried to make sushi. How hard can it be? I grabbed a jar of the RiceSelect Sushi Rice, which purports to be "100% all-natural Koshihikari rice" and took it home with me.

In the kitchen, per the instructions on the label, I started off by rinsing the rice. I put two cups of rice in a stainless-steel bowl, filled the bowl with cold water, and kept the water running as I swished the rice around with my slowly freezing hand. First the water became cloudy, but after several minutes of rinsing and swishing, it ran clear. In the traditional Japanese sushi apprenticeship system one can spend years washing rice, trimming leaves, and mopping floors before graduating to doing anything with actual fish.

I then hauled out my trusty Zojirushi "fuzzy logic" rice cooker. When we got this thing thirteen years ago (it was a prewedding shower gift), it was state-of-the-art. Even Japanese people were impressed that I had one. Today, fuzzy logic is no big deal—not that anyone ever knew what it was—and the rice cooker culture has moved on to induction elements and cooking vessels formed out of single blocks of ceramic. Still, my rice cooker is pretty good. You know it's good because it takes about three times as long to cook rice as it would take just to cook it on the stove. It goes through an elaborate preheating ritual for something like half an hour, then cooks the rice for a normal amount of time, then insists that you not open the lid for about ten minutes after the rice is done cooking. I added water in a water-to-rice ratio of 1.25 to 1 and activated the rice cooker.

Needless to say, once you start cooking rice for sushi, the notion that there's no cooking involved in making sushi falls away.

While this was going on, I watched episode 11 of *Heroes* (as I said, the rice cooker is slow) and searched for the other things I'd need in order to make sushi. In my cabinet I found seasoned rice vinegar. In my refrigerator I had a bottle of soy sauce formulated for sashimi, which I had bought at the H-Mart supermarket in New Jersey (H-Mart is Korean but sells many Japanese products). I then realized I had no wasabi, but I was determined to move forward. I had plenty of horseradish left over from Passover. Why not try it that way?

Eventually the rice was done. I mixed together four tablespoons of seasoned rice vinegar and two tablespoons of white sugar in a little glass, then added that to the rice. I stirred the rice around and fanned it with a magazine (similar to the procedure I've seen in restaurants, though not as effective as an electric fan) in order to incorporate the vinegar and cool the rice a bit. I closed the rice cooker and left it on warm while I plotted my next move.

My wife, Ellen, and son, PJ, were due to arrive home any minute, and they were expecting me to have dinner ready. I decided to set up an improvised sushi bar at the dining room table. I quartered an avocado. I peeled and cut about a quarter of an English hothouse cucumber into little matchsticks. I set out a finger bowl of horseradish and one of cold water, plus a towel, cutting board, and small Japanese knife. I didn't have any sheets of nori, so I wasn't going to be able to make real maki, but I figured I could make a pretend maki with no nori.

I also didn't have one of those wooden mats that are used for rolling maki, so I took a thick black oversized envelope and covered it in plastic wrap, figuring it would at least allow me to roll some rice around a filling.

I was ready to make sushi. As my skeptical family watched (even our bulldog, Momo, seemed to have his doubts), I cut a thin slice of avocado. Then I wet my hands and grabbed some warm rice. I fashioned it into what I thought looked close enough to the correct infrastructure for a piece of nigiri sushi, being careful not to compress it too much. I then put a small amount of horseradish on the rice, picked up the piece of avocado, and cupped it against the rice so that it melded into the whole. I had made my first piece of nigiri sushi. It wasn't pretty, but it was tasty.

I proceeded to make about a dozen of these, passing them out to the family. I'd like to say that my technique improved, but it didn't. I got faster, but every piece of sushi I made was just as ugly as the first. I then moved on to rolls (maki).

My first attempt at maki was a disaster. I had no idea how much rice to use, how much to spread it out, how much filling to use, or how to roll it effectively. I wound up with some pieces of cucumber sitting in the valley of a U-shaped log of rice. I didn't use nearly enough rice, something I'd have figured out if I'd thought about the concept of circumference for a few moments. I tried to patch the roll with some additional rice, but it was beyond repair. On my second attempt, I created a much larger sheet of rice before rolling, and I managed to produce a cylinder of rice with the vegetables near the center.

In the time since that first embarrassing experience, I became skilled enough to make sushi that I'm not ashamed to serve to friends. It's not difficult to make sushi; it's just hard to make *good* sushi. Anybody who doubts that making sushi is real cooking should try making some.

Guerrilla Sushi Tactics

Most restaurants above the level of fast-food and take-out joints, even those that serve some of the lesser-known regional cuisines of Asia, are organized the same way: you sit at a table, you get a menu, you order from a server, and the server brings your food.

At a sushi bar, however, you interact directly with a chef. The chef is your server. (The sushi-bar style is also starting to be emulated in non-sushi restaurants, such as at Joël Robuchon's Atelier, with locations in Paris, New York, and Las Vegas, and the ChikaLicious dessert bar in New York—Western restaurants where customers sit at counters and order directly from chefs.) Getting the most out of a sushi bar therefore requires special tactics.

One thing I learned as a lawyer at a big commercial firm (besides how to bill 3,000 hours a year) was how to look as though I knew what I was doing, even when I didn't. That skill is particularly valuable at sushi bars, because getting the best meal at a sushi bar is all about attitude. Speaking Japanese, of course, helps. Being Japanese is even better, though you don't want to be Japanese and not speak Japanese, because that combination sends you all the way to the bottom of the sushi-bar hierarchy. In any event, I have none of those qualifications, so the ability to project confidence is the only tool available to me. Here's my strategy for extracting the best possible meal.

Sit at the Sushi Bar

There are two types of people eating sushi at a Japanese restaurant: those at the sushi bar, and the tourists. In my experience, sitting at the sushi bar is the single most important thing one can do to improve one's meal at a sushi restaurant. The better the restaurant, the more important this advice becomes. Sitting at the sushi bar won't make mediocre sushi great. But sitting at a table can make a meal at a great sushi restaurant mediocre.

As soon as a piece of sushi is formed, it's a race against time. The best sushi experience happens when the pieces go virtually from the hand of the sushi chef to your mouth. When an individual piece of sushi is crafted, warm rice, cold fish, and the body heat of the sushi chef combine to create body-temperature sushi pieces (called nigiri) that are just right for eating. A few minutes later, the pieces degrade to room temperature and are not nearly as enjoyable. With rolls, soon after the nori and rice make contact, the nori starts to soften and lose its crispness; eventually it becomes soggy and unpleasantly rubbery. Both of these situations are essentially unavoidable when you sit at a table, because the sushi chef will make a platter with your order on it, accumulating the pieces (during which time they deteriorate) before the platter is delivered to your table. If you're at the sushi bar, however, the chef can hand you each piece as soon as it's formed.

In addition, when you're at the sushi bar, you get more information because you deal directly with the sushi chef. You get information not only about what fish are available but also about which are best. At a table, you're dealing with a printed menu and working through the server as an intermediary, and you just don't get the same information.

Sushi chefs cut pieces of varying quality from a single fish. For example, salmon from the middle of the fish is usually better than tail pieces. But a sushi bar, to be profitable, needs to serve the whole salmon. Guess which customers get the less desirable tail pieces? The sushi-bar customers, facing the chef, and facing the fish, usually get the best cuts.

Over the past decade or so, I've heard and read hundreds of comments from people who have dined at the same sushi restaurants but had wildly divergent experiences. The tie that binds so many of those remarks is that the people who dine at the sushi bar overwhelmingly have better experiences than those who dine at the tables. The same restaurant that inspires people to say "best meal I ever had" at the sushi bar can trigger the "I don't see what the big deal is about this place" reaction in those who sit at the tables.

Talk to the Sushi Chef

The sushi chef has a wealth of information that he can share with you, but you have to engage him to get this information. So make eye contact, smile, and start a conversation. And be aware that not all sushi chefs are created equal: at most sushi restaurants, the lead chef (who may even be the owner) stands closest to the restaurant's entrance, with the other chefs positioned down the line in decreasing order of seniority.

Of course you can't expect to start an in-depth conversation, or even to sit in front of the number one sushi chef, on a hectic Saturday night when the restaurant is busy and the chefs are scrambling to keep up with all the sushi-bar, table, and even take-out orders. To build the relationship, it's best to go for lunch, or for an early dinner on an off-night like Tuesday or Wednesday. Go alone, or with just one trusted confederate who can be made to understand and cooperate with the mission. Bring lots of money.

When you arrive at the sushi bar, make eye contact with the sushi chef. Give him (or, in rare instances, her) a quick nod. Try to say with your eyes, "Very serious sushi customer coming your way, chef." Don't try to bow unless you've got proper bowing training, because if you bow too much or too little, you and the chef will get caught in an endless loop of reciprocal bowing and you'll never get any food.

Without being rude, you need to dismiss the waitstaff almost completely. Refuse a menu. Say you're ordering sushi by the piece, and that you're ordering it directly from the chef. Let the waiter bring you some water, some tea, or a beer, but don't let anybody come between you and the sushi chef.

Test the Waters

If you're dining at one of the best sushi restaurants in town, those that have earned their stellar reputations through years of dedication to their customers, you can enter with confidence that the fish will be great. It's not your job to test such restaurants but rather to trust them. At all other sushi restaurants, however, it's caveat emptor: you need to test the waters before diving in.

Announce that you'll be starting with sashimi. Say it as though you know it's obvious that anybody with a clue would start with sashimi. Don't be obnoxious about it—every sushi chef is an experienced amateur psychologist and can spot a poseur clear across the dining room—but project a calm confidence that says you know what you're talking about.

Order two pieces of sashimi: one piece of regular tuna and one piece of toro (belly) tuna. You could perform this test with another fish, such as yellowtail, but in the modern sushi culture tuna is widely considered to be the gold standard and is therefore the most universally worthwhile litmus test. If the restaurant has more than one grade of toro (which is a good sign), you should get the fattiest available for this test. Do not place the rest of your order. Just get those pieces. When they're placed in front of you, eye them very carefully. Look as though you know exactly how to evaluate a piece of sashimi. Pick it up with chopsticks, hold it up, check it out from all angles. Give it some thought. Then eat it, without any soy sauce or wasabi (or, at most, just a tiny bit of each). Reflect deeply as you chew.

If you've done your job right, the sushi chef will be extremely interested to know whether you approved of your tuna. If you did like it, this is the time for a knowing smile. If, however, you think your tuna was lousy, it's time to close the books, cut your losses, pay, and leave. Rest assured, these days it's most likely that there are several other sushi bars within a short distance, even if you live in

Oklahoma City (one of the fastest-growing sushi markets in the United States).

The ability to judge a piece of tuna comes primarily from experience, but the main things you're looking for are a clean taste (which is often described as "fresh," even though the freshest tuna you'll get at even the best sushi restaurant is probably a few days old—don't worry, it will taste fabulous if it's good tuna that has been properly iced); a buttery and fleshy (not mealy) texture; and in the case of the toro, a texture even softer than butter—more like the silken texture of lard. You also want an absence of off-smelling ("fishy") odors, and you want the sushi chef's knife technique to be outstanding—if you can cut a nicer piece of fish yourself, it means the chef is either lazy or incompetent.

If you approve the tuna, order additional sashimi. Finish all your sashimi ordering before you move on to sushi.

Take the Sushi Chef's Advice

Remember, fish isn't a fungible commodity like FCOJ (that's commodities-speak for frozen concentrated orange juice). Even at the best sushi restaurant, not every piece of fish will be at its best every day. Luckily, the sushi chef knows exactly what is best on any given day. So this is the time to ask questions and get advice, and to follow said advice. By now, if you've projected the proper combination of confidence and deference, you'll be in a running conversation with the sushi chef and the information will be flowing.

At an appropriate break in the action, announce, "Now, sushi." This will transition you from the naked raw slices of sashimi to the crosswise slices of the same fish mounted on little lumps of sweetened vinegared rice, or rolled with rice in a seaweed (nori) wrapper. I like to be sure to include regular tuna and toro again here, in order to see the changes they undergo when made into sushi. The warmth of the rice and the subtly different cutting technique used for nigiri sushi combine to give a completely different experience of the exact same food. Also note whether the rice has a little bit of a vinegar taste and a bit of sweetness. It should, but not too much. Proceed to follow the sushi chef's recommendations. After the nigiri sushi, finish up with a roll or two. Try not to squander your credibility by getting a California roll—go for yellowtail-and-scallion, or again solicit some suggestions. Skip dessert, request the check, pay the check (which may be staggering), and tip a normal amount.

Develop the Relationship

If you've decided that this sushi chef is someone you want to work with and learn from (this is like choosing a psychoanalyst, so a good fit is important), ask the chef his name, tell him yours (or earnestly present a business card with both hands), and give him a separate gratuity—a crisp $20 bill will do (unless he's the owner, in which case no tip is necessary). It's also proper etiquette to buy the sushi chef a beer as a sign of appreciation. Go back soon to reinforce his memory of you (when you make the reservation, say "I'd like to sit at the sushi bar with [insert name here]," but this time allow him to choose all your fish (*omakase*).

Now you have your very own personal sushi chef, and there's no reason ever to go to any other sushi restaurant unless he gets a new job (in which case, your loyalty is to the sushi chef, not the establishment). Now you're ready to take dates, friends, and business associates—even Japanese-speaking Japanese ones—out for sushi.

OPPOSITES SUBTRACT: RED WINE WITH SUSHI?

Twenty years ago, Daisuke Utagawa had a revelation over a bowl of gumbo. The son of a Japanese journalist who was a collector of Burgundy wines, Utagawa had been schooled in both Japan and Maryland, and later studied traditional cuisine with Japanese masters. In 1983 he took a job as a sushi chef at the venerable Sushi-Ko restaurant in Washington, D.C. Soon after, at a party in Texas, his host sprinkled raw scallops and shrimp into a bowl of gumbo in the final moments of cooking. Utagawa, who had been sipping a red Burgundy, had a bite of gumbo, and then a sip of wine.

Now the owner of Sushi-Ko, Utagawa has devoted his professional career to making the argument for the marriage of red Burgundy and Japanese cuisine, particularly raw fish. It has not been an easy road, but he has made significant progress.

Utagawa's basic argument is that the tannins in pinot noir (the grape upon which red Burgundy wines are based) are the ideal foil for the *umami* flavor that typifies much raw seafood and Japanese cuisine in general. Umami, often referred to as the fifth taste, is hard to pin down. Sometimes described as "savory" or "meaty," umami is more of an enhancer of flavors that are already in a dish: a quality rather than a taste. To Utagawa's way of thinking, the umami flavors and the tannins interact with each other in what is essentially a mutual subtraction, thus allowing the palate to thoroughly enjoy the fruit flavors of the wine. He also believes that, in their space, the pinot noir tannins shape and define the elusive umami and make it more comprehensible to the taster.

Not entirely satisfied with the inroads he was making in Washington and in the media, Utagawa decided to go to Burgundy to argue his case. With the help of the wine exporter Becky Wasserman, who hosted Utagawa and several leading Burgundy winemakers at a dinner at her seventeenth-century home in Bouilland, he presented his cuisine in combination with Burgundy reds.

Utagawa left Burgundy triumphant, with the support of many key industry figures. He has since made annual pilgrimages to the region, where more and more winemakers are becoming familiar with his theories as he pairs Japanese dishes with their favorite wines.

A while back, I had the opportunity to dine with Utagawa at a meal prepared by Sushi-Ko's current head chef, Koji Terano (Utagawa today devotes his efforts to managing the restaurant and traveling for culinary and oenological research purposes). Peter Wasserman, Becky's son, was on hand with an avalanche of red Burgundies from the Selection Becky Wasserman portfolio.

As I steeled myself in preparation for testing Utagawa's theories against my own palate and sensibilities, I reflected on the number of artificially forced pairings I've endured over the years. A particularly painful red-wine-and-chocolate tasting event a few years back convinced me only that going to such dinners is a high-risk activity: not only do you have to contend with potentially unpleasant food, but if you're forthright in your commentary, you wind up looking industry people straight in the eye and telling them you think they've failed. And while I am no staunch traditionalist in matters of wine, I do have a fairly difficult-to-surmount threshold of credibility when it comes to novelty pairings.

The eel tatsuta-age looked like a good dish: squares of eel, battered and fried like tempura and drizzled with a balsamic syrup, were accompanied by a bright, acidic cucumber salad. And it *was* a good dish, but the moment of truth was still to come: tasting this dish with Domaine Sylvain Pataille Marsannay la Montagne 2001.

I was a convert after one sip. Although I developed some reservations about the enterprise later in the meal, there was no question upon this first taste of umami-rich eel with a young, fruity Burgundy that more was going on than just an acceptable pairing. The tannin-derived synergy that Utagawa promises can easily be detected by even a casual taster, and this seemed to be the mood around the whole table. I found myself settling in, as I alternated bites of eel and sips of Marsannay, to one of the most sensuous wine experiences I can remember.

Some marriages were less successful. I got an unpleasant metallic hit off the pairing of the suimono (a clear broth with whitefish), yamaimo, and egg whites with Domaine Fougeray de Beauclair Bonnes Mares 2000. I couldn't get past it.

Throughout the meal, Utagawa thoroughly impressed me with his seemingly endless knowledge of fish, wine, and everything in between. He held forth about the freezing and storage of fish; he is keenly interested in aquaculture; he has developed relationships with many farmers; and he has created a whole language of colors and symbols that he uses to make his written tasting notes. He has traveled and talked shop with chefs ranging from Ferran Adrià of El Bulli in Roses, Spain, to Kenichi Hashimoto of Ryozanpaku in Kyoto. He has a thorough intellectual concept of a minimalist "cuisine of subtraction" that he strives to implement at Sushi-Ko.

At the end of the meal, I ran through my notes with Utagawa, making my presentation as frank and clear as possible. (Most food writers, I have found, will clam up when faced with industry people and will save their criticisms for the safer medium of print; I don't believe in writing what I wouldn't say directly to a chef, restaurateur, publicist, or producer.) Utagawa processed my critique, and concluded that he felt I could, albeit with some difficulty, be educated.

Beyond Sushi: Taking in the full scope of Japanese cuisine

In North America, sushi has been by far the most successful Japanese culinary import of recent decades. However, Japanese cuisine extends far beyond sushi. In fact, the scope of Japanese cuisine is dizzying, with dozens of categories of food, each with its own traditions wrapped around nuances. In Japan, where specialization is the norm, foods like tempura, noodles, and even single ingredients like eel have their own dedicated restaurants, which tend to be tiny. This specialization explains why there are about ten times as many restaurants in Tokyo as in New York.

By contrast, the Japanese restaurant menu commonly seen in North America combines many different strands of Japanese food and offers them under one roof. Needless to say, the quality of any given offering is likely to be better if made by a specialist. In some of the larger North American cities, there are restaurants dedicated to noodles and other specific non-sushi Japanese foods, and the quality differential is usually apparent.

To get a handle on the world of nonsushi Japanese food, I asked my friend Raji to take me on a tour of specialty restaurants around New York City. Since I was paying, Raji was happy to oblige. It was quite a tour, but first a little about Raji.

Raji isn't Japanese. He isn't really anything. Born in Yonkers, New York, to an Indian father (his last name is Krishnaswami) and a Jewish mother who had both been disowned by their families for intermarrying, Raji grew up culturally agnostic. A few Japanese families had moved to his town, however, and because Raji was the best student at the local public school, he was assigned to be a big sibling to several new Japanese students over the years. He was paired with boys, but they had sisters . . .

Raji's strongest cultural affiliation is now with Japan. He's fluent in Japanese and has lived and worked in Japan on and off for a total of about four years. Raji is a bit of a lost soul, as I've found is not uncommon with expatriates, and has done a little bit of everything: he went to film school, has worked as a DJ, worked for Japanese TV stations, and has started businesses ranging from web design to "bachelor party organizer."

Most of all, Raji loves to eat, and to talk about eating. His number one piece of advice: "I do most of my eating at lunch," Raji advises. "There's a very strong Japanese tradition of offering good-value business lunches. The same restaurants that can cost fifty or a hundred dollars per person at dinnertime may offer lunch specials for ten or twenty dollars. It's a great way to sample what the restaurant has to offer without committing a lot of financial resources."

Our lunchtime route, which continued into the evening, took us to Aburiya Kinnosuke (a favorite business-lunch spot centered around a robata grill, similar in appearance to a sushi bar, but instead they roast meats behind the bar), Menchanko Tei (a ramen noodle soup specialist), Suibi (which has a special menu of Okinawan dishes), Riingo (a modern American-and-Japanese concept with a chef, Marcus Samuelsson, who was born in Ethiopia and raised in Sweden), Saka Gura (an izakaya, kind of like a Japanese tapas bar and jazz club, in an office-building basement), and Setagaya (another ramen specialist).

Watching Raji in action at a Japanese restaurant is a

bit like watching a professional tennis player serve: you know you can never acquire that level of skill, but you can still learn a lot by observing. And I've learned a lot from Raji.

WHEN YOU STEP INTO a Japanese-owned Japanese restaurant, you're stepping into a piece of Japan. So you've got to behave as you'd behave in a foreign country: be respectful of the culture and generally follow the "when in Rome" rule.

One of the realities of Japanese culture is that it's less flexible than North American culture. Americans and Canadians are used to being able to ask for everything "on the side" at a restaurant, everything made a special way. Japan is tradition-oriented. Dishes are made a certain way because that's how they've always been made. If you want to endear yourself to a Japanese restaurant, don't try to have it your way—have it the Japanese way. Luckily, that's usually the best way anyway.

It's helpful to learn just a few words of restaurant Japanese, as a sign of respect. This isn't about convincing restaurant workers that you speak Japanese. It's just a nice way to show that you're interested, that you believe in the culture. For example, *hai* (pronounced "high") means "yes" in Japanese. If your server asks if you'd like water and the answer is yes, try smiling and saying *"hai!"* As a sign of respect, it's polite to add the suffix -*san* to a sushi chef's name. So if his name is Shin, you can refer to him as "Shin-san." Anybody who has listened to Styx knows that *domo arigato* means "thank you very much." And if you really want to get a smile out of the staff at a Japanese restaurant, try saying *Go chi so sama deshita!* as you leave (it means "thanks for the delicious meal").

Of course, Japanese phrases are relevant only if you're speaking to Japanese people. Most Japanese restaurants in North America aren't Japanese-owned. You can often tell the Japanese ones by the Japanese-language newspapers and flyers piled up in the vestibule. Or you can just ask the staff where they're from.

The following are the non-sushi Japanese foods you're most likely to encounter in Japanese restaurants in North America.

Tempura

Deep frying wasn't a cooking technique in Japan until the arrival of Portuguese missionaries in the sixteenth century. Perhaps because it's fundamentally a Western import, tempura is easily accessible to Westerners. Chances are, your friend who doesn't eat Japanese food will at least enjoy tempura.

Tempura refers to battered and deep-fried strips and slices of meat, fish, and vegetables. Most restaurants that offer tempura offer at least the choice of shrimp or chicken tempura, each combined with several different vegetables, such as broccoli, asparagus, zucchini, eggplant, onion, and sweet potato. Many of these vegetables are American adaptations; you'd have very different choices in Japan.

Tempura is usually served alone, with just a couple of condiments. The dipping sauce that accompanies tempura is called *tentsuyu* sauce and is a mix of soy sauce, mirin (sweet rice wine), and dashi (a broth based on kelp and dried tuna flakes). Grated daikon radish is also usually provided. Sometimes tempura is part of another dish, though. *Tempura soba* (also called *tensoba*) refers to tempura served over soba (buckwheat) noodles. *Tendon* is a bowl of rice topped with tempura. And there's also the curious practice of serving *tempura udon,* which is tempura (usually shrimp) served floating on top of a bowl of noodle soup (yes, it immediately becomes soggy).

In Japan, restaurants called *tempura-ya* are devoted entirely to tempura, and are often constructed along the lines of a sushi bar, where the tempura chef stands facing the customers and fries pieces of tempura to order. When cooked properly, tempura is the lightest, least greasy fried food imaginable. Unfortunately, most tempura served in Japanese restaurants in North America isn't particularly good.

Noodles

The three types of Japanese noodle dishes most commonly seen in North America are *soba, udon,* and *ramen.*

Soba noodles, based on buckwheat flour, are the most uniquely Japanese type of noodle. They're similar in thickness to spaghetti and are often served cold with *tsuyu,* a dipping sauce based on soy sauce, mirin, and dashi. Garnishes include wasabi, scallions, and grated ginger. There are also several hot soba preparations, served in broth. Most restaurants serve prepackaged, factory-made soba, but there are a few places that make soba by hand. They're worth seeking out.

Udon noodles are big, fat, soft, and made from white flour. A typical menu will offer a few choices, all hyphenated with the word *udon.* The minimalist version is *kake-udon,* which is simply a hot plain noodle soup. The most elaborate version is *nabeyaki-udon,* which is a soup piled high with assorted vegetables and other ingredients such as fried shrimp, fish cake, egg, and even chicken. *Tempura-udon* combines noodles with tempura (most often shrimp) in soup. Also look for *kitsune-udon* (with fried tofu) and *tororo-udon* (with grated sweet potato).

In North America ramen noodles are commonly identified with the ten-for-a-dollar packages of instant ramen, with a packet of salty artificial flavor enclosed, consumed by college students on tight budgets. Those products are a far cry from good ramen, which some of the better restaurants elevate to a complex, subtle cuisine unto itself. Ramen noodles are based on wheat flour and mineral-rich water. They can come in several formats; the most common shape is similar to angel-hair pasta. Broths can be made from pork, chicken, seafood, or a combination thereof, and a wide range of ingredients can be added to the soup. Dedicated ramen shops can be found in larger North American cities. They tend to be open late—ramen is one of the best foods to enjoy after a night of drinking. Ramen shops are also often the best places to get *gyoza*, the delicate Japanese dumplings.

In Japan it has long been considered proper etiquette to slurp one's noodles loudly. The slurping-sucking maneuver cools the noodles on the way from the soup bowl to your mouth. No Japanese person is going to be surprised if you slurp your noodles, even though it's not a widespread practice in the West, where slurping in general is frowned upon. (Even in Japan, noodle-slurping is said to be on the decline.)

Sukiyaki

One of the first Japanese dishes to gain popularity in North America, sukiyaki is a popular soup served in an iron pot. In a few restaurants it's served as a cook-it-yourself hot pot, but at most it's presented as a completed dish. The main ingredients are usually thin strips of beef (some restaurants offer chicken or pork as well) in a broth based on soy sauce, sugar, and mirin, and garnished with tofu, scallions, cabbage, mushrooms, and clear noodles. Sukiyaki is especially warming in winter and is a good starter dish for people who are hesitant about trying Japanese food.

Teriyaki

Teriyaki preparations appeal to American palates, largely because they're sweet. As a result, bottled teriyaki sauces are one of the most popular Japanese items available in mainstream supermarkets. These bottled sauces are gloppy and cloying compared to higher-quality teriyaki sauces made by good restaurants. The basic elements of teriyaki sauce are soy sauce, rice wine, and sugar. In Japan teriyaki preparations are seafood-oriented, but in North America meat is king. Teriyaki items are grilled, and the teriyaki sauce is applied several times throughout the cooking process. Well-made teriyaki items come out shiny in appearance (the word *teriyaki* comes from *teri,* which refers to shine or luster) and sweet, but not overwhelmingly so.

Donburi

A complete meal in a bowl, traditionally eaten for lunch, donburi consists of a bowlful of steamed white rice covered with toppings such as chicken, pork, or tempura. Restaurants that offer donburi usually offer them only on their lunch menus, though I'd happily eat donburi for breakfast and dinner too.

The names of donburi dishes are usually written without hyphens—the *don* is simply employed as a suffix. So, for example, donburi topped with raw tuna is *tekkadon.* Several variations on donburi are found on restaurant menus:

Katsudon: topped with deep-fried breaded meat cutlet (usually pork) and egg. Chicken may also be offered as an option. Also look for *katsu curry* (topped with the same kind of cutlet but with a thick brown curry sauce), or *curry rice* (just the rice and sauce).

Oyakodon: topped with chicken and egg (the name refers to "parent and child")

Tendon: topped with tempura

Unadon: topped with broiled eel

Miso soup

Miso soup is an afterthought in the minds of many American diners; it's something that's included in the dinner combination special at a Japanese restaurant. But in Japanese food culture, miso soup is almost as central as rice. A substantial portion of the Japanese population eats miso soup every day—for breakfast.

Miso soup is a combination of two key Japanese ingredients: *dashi* and *miso*. In Western cookery, stocks are made by slowly simmering bones and meat to extract their flavor. The foundational Japanese stock, dashi, comes at it from a different angle: a type of kelp called *kombu* and thin shavings of dried bonito (skipjack tuna, called *katsuobushi* in Japanese) are quickly boiled in water and then strained out, leaving behind a flavorful stock that tastes of the sea. Miso is a salty, robustly flavored paste created through an elaborate fermentation process. It starts out as soybeans, rice, or barley (or a combination) and a mold called *kojikin*, plus a lot of salt. Miso paste is used in a wide range of Japanese food applications, from pickling to sauces.

When dashi and miso are combined, they create a nourishing, delicious soup. Miso soup can take many forms, but the typical little bowl included with the restaurant meal usually contains small cubes of tofu and sometimes seaweed. Miso soup is usually served in little lacquered bowls. You'll probably be given a spoon, but the bowls are meant to be picked up; you're supposed to drink the soup directly from the bowl and then eat the solid ingredients with chopsticks.

SPECIALTY RESTAURANTS

Aside from the general-menu Japanese restaurants, several other types of Japanese restaurants can be found in North America.

Teppanyaki

Teppanyaki restaurants, often called Japanese steakhouses or hibachi steakhouses, were popularized in North America by the Benihana chain, which opened its first restaurant here in 1964. *Teppan* means "iron plate" and *yaki* means "grilled," and in teppanyaki restaurants various meats, fish, vegetables, and even noodles are prepared on a griddle in front of the customers. Watching the teppanyaki chef perform is half the attraction, and because the tables are built around the griddles, they tend to be large. So you'll often sit and eat with strangers, which can be great fun. Although teppanyaki can be delicious, it would be unfortunate for a teppanyaki restaurant to be someone's only exposure to Japanese cuisine. Teppanyaki is atypical and doesn't quite capture the Japanese aesthetic of understated minimalism.

Kaiseki

Kaiseki meals are lengthy, formal, multicourse meals. There aren't many kaiseki restaurants in North America, but there are a few, and the meals they serve are astounding. Multiple small plates are served in a progression, and the bill is likely to be large. Many believe that the kaiseki tradition influenced French chefs in the 1960s and '70s and was an inspiration for the nouvelle cuisine movement, when minimalism and multicourse tasting menus became popular in France and beyond.

Izakaya

Izakaya is Japan's answer to the tapas bar. People go to an izakaya to drink sake, beer, whiskey, wine, and cocktails, to listen to music (often live jazz), and to graze on small plates of food. Izakaya is one of the hottest trends in Japanese food in North America right now, and is particularly popular in Vancouver. Izakaya food is diverse and can include scaled-down versions of almost any style of Japanese food. Common izakaya menu items include sashimi (sushi is less common), yakitori (grilled skewers of chicken), karaage (fried chicken nuggets), and tofu (especially agedashi tofu, which is deep-fried tofu in soup).

Shabu-shabu

Shabu-shabu is a Japanese hot pot dish, where thin slices of raw meat and vegetables are cooked in a simmering broth at the table. (Shabu-shabu restaurants typically have gas burners built into the tables.) After heating in the broth, the pieces are dipped in a sauce and eaten with rice. Unlike the sweet broth of sukiyaki, shabu-shabu broth is mildly flavored. As the meat and vegetables are cooked in it, however, the broth picks up flavor; the broth is customarily eaten with the last of the white rice at the end of the meal.

PREGNANT SUSHI

When my wife was pregnant with our son, her obstetrician gave her a list of food "dos and don'ts." Chief among the don'ts: alcohol, unpasteurized cheese, and raw fish. Every French mother I know consumed alcohol and unpasteurized cheese in moderation during her pregnancy, and my friends in Japan laugh at the notion of avoiding sushi when they're expecting.

Indeed, in Japan, eating raw fish is considered part of good neonatal nutrition. The Japanese government is fanatical about public health, and Japanese medical scientists are among the best in the world. You can be sure that, were there documented complications resulting from pregnant women eating sushi in Japan, there would be swift government intervention.

Yet in the United States, it is taboo for a pregnant woman to eat raw fish. A pregnant woman seen eating any sushi other than a California roll or a cucumber roll will be summarily tried and convicted by her peers: she is clearly a delinquent mother.

But this isn't because scientific research has concluded that unborn children have been damaged by sushi. Rather, it's because the speculative risk of food-borne illnesses, especially parasites, has captured the public imagination.

There are several reasons, however, why these fears are unfounded.

While Americans tend to associate raw fish with

sushi and Japan, we have been eating raw seafood for centuries—namely, oysters and clams. And it is these raw mollusks, not the fish typically used in sushi, that are responsible for the overwhelming majority (about 85 percent) of seafood-related illnesses. As the National Academy of Sciences (NAS) concluded in a 1991 report on illness from eating seafood: "Most seafood-associated illness is reported from consumers of raw bivalve mollusks. . . . The majority of incidents are due to consumption of shellfish from fecally polluted water."

If you take raw and partly cooked shellfish out of the equation, the risk of falling ill from eating seafood is one in 2 million servings, the U.S. government calculated some years back; by comparison, the risk from eating chicken is one in 25,000. (Overall, 76 million cases of food poisoning are reported each year in the United States alone.)

The main risk of illness from nonmollusks isn't from eating them raw. Rather, as the NAS reports, the problem is "cross-contamination of cooked by raw product," which is "usually associated with time/temperature abuse." In other words, no matter what you order in a restaurant, if it's not kept at a proper temperature and protected from contamination, you're at risk.

Conversely, if the restaurant follows good food safety practices, there is little to worry about. Having been inside the kitchens of dozens of restaurants of all kinds, I can say that Japanese kitchens are, on the whole, the cleanest in the business and the staff is the most careful and the most conscientious. Moreover, sushi bars are out in the open for all to see, and anybody who has spent a few minutes observing a sushi bar and a typical American diner's griddle area can tell you which type of restaurant has higher standards of cleanliness.

Sushi may not be cooked, but it has, for the most part, been frozen. Food and Drug Administration guidelines require that before being served as sushi or sashimi (or in any other raw form), fish be flash-frozen to destroy parasites. While the fish you see in the sushi-bar display case looks fresh, it has almost certainly been frozen at some point in the distribution system. This freezing kills any parasites as surely as cooking would.

Most species used for sushi don't have parasites anyway, though. Fish like tuna are not particularly susceptible to parasites because they dwell in very deep, very cold water; and sushi restaurants typically use farmed salmon to avoid the parasite problems wild salmon have. Most of the fish likely to have parasites, like cod and whitefish, aren't generally used for sushi. As the NAS observes: "Seafood-related parasitic infections are even less common than bacterial and viral infections. . . . In general, parasitic infections have resulted from consumption of raw or partially cooked fresh- and salt-water fish of particular species (e.g., whitefish, salmon)."

Nor does pregnancy increase susceptibility to parasites, bacteria, or viruses. Healthy women who've been eating sushi are not at increased risk when they become pregnant. The same resistance and immunities function before, during, and after pregnancy.

But rational analysis doesn't hold sway with the self-appointed pregnancy police.

"Why take any risk?" they ask. The medical establishment and the culture at large have twisted logic around to the point where any risk, no matter how infinitesimal, is too much. So powerful is this puritanical impulse that once a health objection is raised, however irrational the recommended behavior, it's considered irresponsible to behave any other way.

There's a temptation to say there's no harm in this type of thinking. Women should simply not eat sushi for nine months; surely that's no big deal. But there are problems with this approach.

For one thing, between the warnings about parasites in sushi and about mercury in certain species of fish, pregnant women are being scared off fish altogether. And that's bad news, since the fatty acids in fish are the ideal nourishment for a developing baby. An observational study of more than 8,000 pregnant women and their children, reported in the British journal *The Lancet*, showed that the children whose mothers ate less than twelve ounces of seafood per week were approximately 45 percent more likely to be in the lowest 25 percent of IQ test takers.

For another thing, the sushi ban is insulting to Japanese culture. It speaks of ignorance and prejudice to reject one of that culture's basic foods based on unfounded health claims.

And perhaps most important, pregnancy should be a time of joy, not stress. The result of an overregulated pregnancy is fear and negativity. Perhaps the best antidote would be to relax with a salmon roll and a nice sake.

CHAPTER 2

Chinese

Good Luck in Cleveland: Great Chinese food lives in a strip mall

Turn left at the Kentucky Fried Chicken" isn't exactly the way I expected to be directed to one of America's finest Chinese restaurants. Then again, I didn't imagine it would be in a strip mall in Cleveland either.

Sun Luck Garden used to be a Little Caesars pizzeria. Down toward one end of a shopping center that's seen better days, from the outside it's difficult to tell if the restaurant is even open. Inside it's somewhat more elegant, but there's certainly nothing to indicate that you've entered a great restaurant. Not even the menu provides much in the way of hints. That's because many of the best dishes aren't on the menu—you have to ask for them.

The campaign to meet Annie Chiu, chef-owner of Sun Luck Garden in Cleveland Heights, Ohio, began weeks in advance. Michael Ruhlman, by far the foremost food writer living anywhere near Cleveland, made the connection for me.

Eventually, after clearing a background check more rigorous than anything the FBI would demand, I'm granted an audience. Annie Chiu is waiting in the parking lot when I arrive. She ushers me into the kitchen, where her two cooks are prepping for the lunch service. The pace is methodical, relaxed. Annie is making desserts. In complete defiance of Chinese-restaurant stereotypes, Sun Luck Garden is known for its desserts, so much so that some people come in after dinner elsewhere just for Annie's cheesecake with plum sauce, or peach almond cake, or whatever she happens to be making that day.

During the lunch service, Annie waits on all the tables and her two cooks prepare the food. At 11:59 A.M., Annie and I are chatting pleasantly, but as soon as the clock strikes 12:00 she stops midsentence and announces, "I have to work RIGHT NOW!"

As soon as Annie calls the first orders into the kitchen, the two cooks, Henry and Ken, explode in a frenzy of activity. Woks, cleavers, and ladles are flying everywhere, almost too fast to see. In a war, I speculate, these two guys could probably confuse the enemy by pretending to be an entire platoon. I'm exhausted just watching for the ninety or so minutes that the lunch service lasts.

To someone familiar mostly with Western European–derived cooking, a Chinese-restaurant kitchen can be disorienting. Everything is just a little different: different knives, different cookware, different ideas of ergonomics, time, and motion. For example, Chinese-restaurant stoves are built with faucets right over them. That way, to clean a wok, the cook doesn't even have to walk away from the stove. He just turns on the faucet, brushes the wok clean, and dumps the water into a drainage channel that's integrated into the design of the stove. It's so efficient, there isn't even a knob on the faucet; rather, the act of swinging the faucet out from the wall turns on the water, and pushing it back shuts the water off. The process is so seamless that there's never any real interruption in the parade of dishes being cooked.

And Chinese-restaurant cooks work hard. I've been in dozens of American and European kitchens and these two guys at Sun Luck Garden make even the hardest-working Western cooks look like lightweights.

I've eaten more than my fair share of egg foo yung in my life, but for the first time I get to see it made. Annie explains, in between clearing tables and taking orders, that bean sprouts—the key ingredient in egg foo yung—were one of the few Chinese-style vegetables that early Chinese-American immigrants had access to. Because they grow indoors, in dark places, they're easy to cultivate in basements, garages, and closets. To make the egg foo yung, Henry takes a small saucepan and uses it as a mixing bowl. He first adds a fistful of bean sprouts. Using an inverted aluminum can as a circular blade, he chops the bean sprouts into little pieces. Then he cracks in an egg, mixes, and adds various vegetables. He forms the resulting batter into three patties with a flat ladle-like tool and slips each patty into hot oil in a wok. After a couple of minutes, he turns the patties. When they're done, two of them go on a plate for the customer and one goes on a plate for me. Henry covers each patty with a brown gravy.

It's the best egg foo yung I've ever tasted. Normally a greasy mess, this egg foo yung is light and airy, and the gravy reminds me of what my mother's Thanksgiving turkey gravy would have tasted like had I grown up in a

Chinese family—except this gravy contains no meat. Because Sun Luck Garden is in a heavily Jewish neighborhood, Annie has designed many of the menu items to be vegetarian, or at least free of pork and shellfish.

Annie Chiu's path to Chinese-restaurant ownership isn't the typical immigrant story. She came to America from Hong Kong at age seventeen to attend university on the West Coast and originally thought she'd go into finance. She got interested in cooking while in college, primarily as a means of feeding herself. In Cleveland, before opening Sun Luck Garden in 1993, she spent more than a decade working in different kinds of kitchens, including the best French and Italian restaurants in town. That's where she picked up, among other things, her pastry skills.

Sun Luck Garden specializes in the same dishes served at the average Westernized Chinese restaurant, but with better ingredients, a lighter hand, and superior skill. About a year after my first visit, I returned with a group of acquaintances and we tasted all the Chinese-restaurant standards: egg rolls, dumplings, cold sesame noodles, fried rice, and more. Each was a revelation of subtle, pure flavors. For example, Annie's cold sesame noodles have just the thinnest, translucent glaze of sesame sauce on them and are enhanced by thin slivers of mushrooms.

But while all the dishes I've tried from the Sun Luck Garden menu have been quite good, the real action is off the menu. Each day there are specials, based on what strikes Annie's fancy. It could be a whole fish or a special purchase of mussels. Whatever it is, customers in the know often don't even look at the menu.

Beyond the daily specials, though, is another level of insider dishes. Annie keeps a list of regular customers who have expressed an interest in special foods, and she calls the people on her list whenever she has an interesting item to offer. It might be a Sino-French theme dinner, or foie gras with Chinese spices for New Year's Eve, or even, if she's in the mood, Italian night. Italian night, at a Chinese restaurant? "If food is good, it's good," Annie lectures me. "It doesn't matter if it's American, Chinese, Italian, even French. If it's good, it's good. Good food is good. Why do we have to brand everything?" I ask Annie why she doesn't offer these special dishes to everyone. "Because they don't want to pay," she says. "They want Chinese food to be cheap. So I give them the best I can for what they want to pay. I'm not going to try to sell a twenty-dollar dish to someone who comes in wanting to pay seven dollars."

By the end of the day, Annie is treating me more like a family member than a journalist. "Why didn't you bring your wife?" she wants to know. "Let me send you home with some desserts for her." Given the number of desserts Annie packs up, it's a good thing we have a minivan.

GOOD FORTUNE IN NEW YORK

HELP! I'M TRAPPED IN A FORTUNE COOKIE FACTORY!

On March 30, 2005, there were 110 second-place winners in the Powerball lottery. Every one of them chose the same five numbers: 22, 28, 32, 33, and 39. This unexpected coincidence led to $19.4 million in unanticipated payouts to the winners.

At first, it seemed clear that a conspiracy to commit fraud had to be responsible for the situation.

The statistical likelihood of 110 people picking the same five numbers is so low as to be unimaginable. Upon investigation, however, a surprising explanation came to light: the fortune cookie was to blame.

It turned out that the "lucky numbers" in a production run of several thousand fortune cookies manufactured by Wonton Food Inc. of Long Island City, Queens, were indeed lucky. And 110 Chinese-restaurant customers who got a fortune cookie with those lucky numbers played the same five numbers in Powerball. The fortune, by the way, was "All the preparation you've done will finally be paying off."

Fortune cookies have worked their way into popular culture. They appear everywhere, from the Joy Luck Club, to websites like Weird Fortune Cookie (weirdfortunecookies.com), to the 1960s film *The Fortune Cookie* with Walter Matthau and Jack Lemmon (directed by Billy Wilder, this was the first-ever film this famous pair of actors did together). Superstitions abound: a double fortune is good luck; a broken cookie is bad luck. They are the tie that binds most every Chinese-restaurant experience in North America.

And fortune cookies go beyond the Chinese restaurant. Marriage proposals delivered in fortune cookies are not unheard of, and custom-printed fortune cookies at weddings, bar mitzvahs, and sweet sixteens are popular enough to support several manufacturers. At the hyper-modern avant-garde Spanish restaurant Minibar, in

Washington, D.C., the check is presented inside a fortune cookie formed just moments before. Fortune cookies have even been used in political campaigns.

Nobody knows exactly why fortune cookies have won over American hearts and minds, but for me, personally, it's simply because they're so much fun.

YOU LOVE CHINESE FOOD.

The fortune cookie, contrary to what many people assume, is not Chinese—a Californian invention. Although there are conflicting accounts of its exact origin, it has been pinpointed to either San Francisco or Los Angeles in the first decades of the twentieth century, and perhaps to Japan before then. In a mock trial in 1983, San Francisco won the argument; however, posttrial accusations of bias (the judge was from San Francisco) have rendered the verdict suspect.

Today the leading manufacturer, the aforementioned Wonton Food Inc., produces 4 million cookies a day (under the "Golden Bowl" brand), operates twenty-four hours a day, seven days a week, and supplies a network of four hundred wholesale distributors in North America and beyond (Panama, Portugal, Greece). There are even variations in flavoring: on the East Coast, citrus is the preferred flavor; in the Midwest, vanilla.

Fortune cookies were made by hand, painstakingly, using chopsticks, until 1964, when Edward Louie of the Lotus Fortune Cookie Company in San Francisco engineered a machine to fold the dough and insert the fortune. Recently, fortune cookies have started to come individually wrapped in plastic.

There may be a Chinese historical precedent for the fortune cookie: the moon cake. Legend has it that during the Mongol occupation of China, revolutionaries hid secret messages inside moon cakes. The tradition doesn't seem to have followed through to modern China, though. When Wonton Food Inc. opened a factory in China in 1994, it was a failure and quickly went out of business.

THE RUBBER BANDS ARE HEADING IN THE RIGHT DIRECTION.

Fortune cookies became especially popular after World War II, when many soldiers from the Pacific theater experienced them while on leave in California. At that time, fortune cookies contained mostly aphorisms from Confucius, as well as Biblical sayings and historical quotations. Over the course of the latter half of the twentieth century, fortune-cookie writing diversified and grew to include everything from humor to outright incomprehensible weirdness. In addition, fortune cookies started to include lucky numbers, smiley faces, and "learn Chinese" vocabulary lessons.

In the modern era, the most influential writer of fortunes has been Donald Lau, the accounts payable manager at Wonton Food Inc. In the 1980s, when Wonton Food bought the factory that is now the global epicenter of fortune-cookie production, Lau was drafted to write the fortunes. He told the *New*

Yorker magazine: "I was chosen because my English was the best of the group, not because I'm a poet."

For a decade, Lau wrote three or four new fortunes a day. Since 1995 he has mostly recycled the greatest hits. Rumor has it that Wonton Food will soon hire a new fortune-cookie writer, but it shouldn't be hard to find one: Lau's e-mail in-box fills up daily with the résumés of his potential successors.

Chinese-Americans and American-Chinese Cuisine: A tale of two menus

It is still the case in many Chinese restaurants in North America, especially in Chinatowns and in suburbs with dense Chinese-American populations, that there are two menus: the one printed in English and automatically handed to anyone with a non-Asian face, and the one in Chinese that's offered to Asians. The two menus do not contain the same list of dishes. In addition, many Chinese restaurants have daily and seasonal specials, sometimes several lists of them, that are offered only to Asian customers.

Don't blame Chinese-restaurant managers for this state of affairs. Blame mainstream North Americans, who have been displaying closed-minded ignorance since the 1840s, when Chinese immigration began in earnest. Chinese restaurants are just giving Western customers what the historical evidence indicates most of them want.

The de facto segregation of Chinese restaurants began as soon as they threw open their doors to Western clients. The first recorded Chinese restaurant in North America, opened in 1849, was San Francisco's Macao and Woosung, operated by a Mr. Norman Asing. During the same period, Chinese restaurants were also springing up in mining towns along the West Coast. White customers, a valuable source of revenue, found the Chinese food at these restaurants disgusting, so the Chinese cooks made whatever they thought would sell. They adapted to meet mainstream palate expectations, while offering a different menu to their Chinese clientele.

In the 1850s most Chinese immigrants couldn't become naturalized Americans; they were instead designated "aliens ineligible for citizenship." They paid taxes and contributed to the economy but had limited rights. They couldn't vote, hold office, own land, file mining claims, or testify in court. In 1882 the United States Congress passed the shameful Chinese Exclusion Act, which begins, "Whereas, in the opinion of the Government of the United States the coming of Chinese laborers to this country endangers the good order of certain localities within the territory thereof," and was the first of a series of laws that severely limited Chinese immigration until the passage of the Immigration Act of 1965.

Though a great moral and political victory, the 1965 act was also one of the great events in U.S. culinary history because it opened the borders to the great cuisines of the world. Chinese master chefs, many of whom had received their training before Communism had taken hold in China, came to America. By the early 1970s, the major American cities were in the midst of a Chinese culinary renaissance, thanks to chefs skilled in Hunan, Sichuan (back then they spelled it "Szechuan" or "Szechwan"), Cantonese, and other regional Chinese cuisines. The renaissance of the 1970s gave way to a period of malaise in the 1980s, as downward pricing pressure from consumers and upward real estate pricing pressure forced many restaurants to close or convert to lowbrow take-out operations.

In the 1990s, during the run-up to the handover of Hong Kong from the British to the Chinese, there was much fear and uncertainty about Hong Kong's future. As a result, Hong Kong investment poured into North America's Chinatowns, triggering a resurgence of serious Chinese cooking, especially in large seafood restaurants like those found in Hong Kong, as well as in fine Shanghai restaurants. Immigration patterns, too, have changed, and the latest wave of Chinese immigrants hails from Fujian province, whose major city is called Fuzhou. Fuzhou cuisine is the trendy Chinese cuisine of the moment, especially on the East Coast.

It remains to be seen whether Chinese cuisine in America has a future as a representative of one of the world's great cuisines, or whether it will be cheapened and dumbed down by consumer expectations (Chinese restaurants have, historically, adapted to the desires of their customers). In the meantime, the smart customer can get a great Chinese meal even at a restaurant that caters primarily to mainstream Westerners. But if you want to order that meal, you first have to overcome the inertia of more than 150 years of bad behavior.

TEMPLE OF TASTE

In Brookline, Massachusetts, an independent hamlet of 58,456 people surrounded by Boston as if by a horseshoe, there are at least fourteen synagogues. But there's only one Temple—that is, the Golden Temple Chinese restaurant. A Boston private eye searching for a missing Jew would be advised to start at Golden Temple, especially on Christmas Eve. For while Christians are hanging their stockings by the chimney with care and digging into Christmas goose, the other half of the Judeo-Christian equation is waiting in a two-hour line to order up Beijing duck.

It's often said that to find the best ethnic restaurants one should look for establishments populated by the corresponding ethnic groups; but in the case of Chinese restaurants, the better strategy may be to listen for conversations about bar mitzvahs and Israeli politics. Nobody knows why these two great civilizations—the Chinese and the Jewish—have come together in the culinary arena. Perhaps there is a natural affinity among the world's most ancient cultures, though some would argue that the Chinese have yet to reciprocate and provide Jewish delis with a significant amount of business. But one thing is certain: American Jews are preeminent consumers of Chinese cuisine.

Or, in the case of Golden Temple, a specific version of Chinese cuisine, which could almost be considered as Jewish as it is Chinese. The menu at

Golden Temple runs the gamut from the traditional to the assimilated and includes dishes like chicken livers with walnuts (Jewish-Chinese fusion), such standards as crispy orange beef and shrimp with lobster sauce, and newfangled, trendy-sounding things like "Chardonnay chicken," "Zinfandel shrimps," and even steak frites.

An old joke popularized by the likes of Jackie Mason runs that Jewish civilization began 6,000 years ago and Chinese civilization 4,000 years ago, and so for 2,000 years the Jews went hungry. At Golden Temple, they're making up for lost time.

Understanding Chinese Restaurants

BEGINNER: GAMING THE CHINESE BUFFET

In much of North America today, the buffet is the most popular entry-level way to experience Chinese cuisine. Like them or not, buffets certainly have their advantages in terms of economy and diversity: for usually less than $10, you get to try as many items as you like (and as much as you like). The drawbacks tend to be lack of freshness (stuff sitting on steam tables for too long) and, often, low quality. To a great extent, however, your fate is in your hands: you may never have a truly excellent Chinese meal at a buffet—for that you'll need to move on to restaurants where your food is cooked to order—but your strategy at the buffet can mean the difference between a bad meal and a very good one.

I started the journey of this book believing that I'd simply exclude buffets from my research. Surely, I thought, they're not serious restaurants. But in town after town it became clear that not only is this form of restaurant dominant but also a buffet can be tasty, a good value, and great fun. The real question isn't "Buffet, yes or no?" but rather, "How do I get the most out of a buffet?"

Here are a few of the strategies I've accumulated, both from my own experience and from tips gathered from buffet die-hard acquaintances (especially those who post to the eG Forums at www.eGullet.org), with the aim of maximizing quality, value, and even nutrition.

Timing Is Key

At any buffet there's a life cycle to the meal. The best time to go is right at the beginning of that cycle, because the food will be at its freshest. If the place opens at 11:30 A.M. for lunch or 5:30 P.M. for dinner, try to go then. Another good time to go is at the peak of the meal service, because there will be the most turnover of food at that time. The worst time to go is toward the end of a meal service, when it's dregs all the way. That's a good time to go out for pizza instead.

Seek the High Ground

Where you sit, and therefore your vantage point, can make a big difference to your success at the buffet. If you can, get a table that has a good view of the part of the buffet containing the hot foods so you can monitor their freshness. It's also helpful to be close, though for comfort's sake you want to be at least one row of tables away from the buffet traffic corridor.

Let the Kitchen Guide Your Meal

Flexibility in the sequencing of your meal is essential. It's not about when you want dumplings. It's about when the fresh, new, hot dumplings come out from the kitchen. Sometimes you're going to get your dumplings at the beginning of the meal, sometimes at the end, and sometimes you have to be willing to dispense with dumplings because the fresh ones just didn't become available while you were in the house. I have, on many occasions, gone back for a freshly replenished savory item even after I've had dessert. Fried foods are always the top priority—they degrade rapidly on the buffet. Dishes of a soupy nature hold up the best—that's what you should be eating during the downtime. Or just take a break and wait.

Many Trips, Small Quantities

Loading up big plates with tons of food—sometimes I see people two-fisting it—is just a bad idea if you want the best of the buffet in the best possible condition. You've got to commit to the idea of making a lot of trips. I think of my first trip or three as mostly exploratory: I'm trying to determine what's good. (If you've been to a given buffet many times before, and the offerings are always the same, you can of course skip this step.) I may very well taste the smallest available portion of every item that isn't self-evidently terrible. There are often surprises. Once I figure out where to focus my eating, I can start prioritizing based on freshness. In some extreme instances, where you find yourself at a buffet that only has two or three good items, take as much as you plan to eat of those when they're fresh and resist the temptation to eat anything else.

Press On to the Way Back

My friend Anne Crosby in Florida offers this advice: "The best food is the most relatively distant from the buffet line that it can get. Don't stumble and fill up on the cheap doorstops, but rather walk to the farthest serving point, and work your way back to the table."

Bigger Is Better

Ellen Terris Brenner, an online acquaintance in San Diego who contributes to the sandiego.eats.it food blog, advises: "At buffets, size definitely does matter—the size of the establishment as a whole, that is. My current favorite here in San Diego seats a huge number of people, and the staff is extremely efficient at replenishing all the food those people Hoover up, resulting in high food turnover and a high degree of freshness during most of their hours of operation." A related point: choose a popular restaurant. Buffets need a critical mass of customers in order to be able to offer a wide variety of good, fresh stuff.

Communicate

Of all my online contacts, the most supremely talented buffet eater is surely Mark in New Jersey. Mark is the Babe Ruth, the Bobby Fischer, and the Wolfgang Amadeus Mozart of the buffet. Not only does he have a superhuman capacity for eating, but he also has the uncanny ability to turn any buffet into his own private bacchanalia. His best piece of advice: "The best way to get the least-plentiful (i.e., premium) items is to ask. And I wouldn't wait a long time to do it either. I mean, if you assume that the lobster or the Peking duck will be coming soon, you may wind up waiting 30 minutes and then wishing you'd asked sooner. And I find that asking the runners does no good whatsoever—they merely carry out what the kitchen prepares. The only thing that helps is to identify a manager (at the larger operations), or the person who seems to be in charge at the smaller ones, and to ask them."

Choose Your Companions Wisely

You should go to a buffet only in the company of people who like to eat as much as you do. In the hierarchy of buffet indignities, nothing tops being rushed out by your friends who just don't care about food, or are on diets, or have someplace they need to be. Getting the most out of the buffet requires the cooperation of the group, a shared sense of purpose, and a mutual understanding that there are no rules: for example, everyone at the table should feel free to get up at any time in order to snag a tasty morsel.

Use a Garbage Plate

An eG Forums participant who goes by the handle "friedclams" turned me on to this trick: "Eating strategy for hot or cold items which have residue of some kind (shells, bones, etc.) must include taking an extra garbage plate back to the table." In other words, in addition to your plate of food, bring back an empty plate for your discards. This simple bit of advice has really improved my enjoyment of buffets, because it allows me to maintain a tidy eating plate and segregate the castoffs.

Limit Carbs

Don't eat a lot of rice, noodles, or other carbohydrate-heavy items unless they're really good. Fried rice and lo mein are rarely all that good, and they fill you up when you could be eating different, better food. (Not to mention the restaurant is hoping you'll fill up on carbs, thus keeping the food cost down.)

THE ABOVE ADVICE IS all you need for most places, but some exceptional buffets require exceptional strategies because they're so elaborate. The most extensive places may have a half-dozen active cooking and carving stations, or special nights when they feature seafood. In such cases, the most useful rule of thumb is that the made-to-order and special items are often (though not always) the best.

I've recommended some aggressive buffet tactics. It's important to remember, though, that getting the most out of a Chinese buffet shouldn't be about gluttony (though it is for too many people). For the smart buffet strategist, the idea isn't to eat as much food as you can but rather to take advantage of the opportunity to try many different dishes—something you can't do at a conventional restaurant unless you're dining with a dozen other people and are willing to spend substantially more money.

Moreover, at the Chinese buffet, good health and good value often go hand in hand. It so happens that many of the most wholesome, nutritious items on the buffet are also the ones that carry the highest food cost: fish and shellfish, fresh vegetables, sushi (a fixture at most big Chinese buffets these days), and simple grilled and made-to-order items. Everybody loves a bargain. Since everybody at a buffet pays the same price, the way you create a bargain is by getting the most for your money. It's a win-win situation. And don't overlook fresh fruit for dessert (most other dessert items are likely to be terrible).

Chinese buffets are not the only Asian buffets out there.

Indian buffets are extremely popular, and we're seeing more and more hybrid pan-Asian buffets offering dishes from Japan, Korea, Southeast Asia, and beyond. All the advice given here applies equally to these other types of buffets.

Remember, a buffet is a system in which the participants exercise a tremendous amount of self-determination. The most facile person at the buffet is going to get the best meal. That person should be you.

FRIED DUMPLING: ALL KINDS OF DUMPLINGS

When people find out I'm a food critic, their immediate reaction (after saying, "Really? I've never heard of you.") is to ask me what my favorite New York restaurants are. They always seem disappointed by my answers, which I confess are nothing more than the usual suspects: the places with three or four *New York Times* stars and strong showings in the Zagat survey.

No, people don't want to hear me say that I like fancy restaurants like Per Se, Jean Georges, Gramercy Tavern, and Nobu. What they really want to hear is "Well, there's this little out-of-the-way place, and only Chinese people and cops eat there, and your whole meal costs a dollar, and the owner used to be the emperor's private chef . . ."

Well, as luck would have it, there is a little out-of-the-way place, and only Chinese people and cops eat there, and your whole meal really does cost a dollar. I can't pretend to know the owner's history because my Chinese-speaking friends report having just as much trouble understanding him in Chinese as I have in English. But, to the extent that loyalty defines a favorite, this place bears the dubious distinction of being the restaurant I visited more times than any other in the past year (more than thirty times, based on my somewhat reliable records).

The restaurant is called Fried Dumpling, or at least those are the only English words on the sign up front. The business card is more descriptive: "Retail and Wholesales; All Kinds of Dumpling." It's hidden away on the Lower East Side of Manhattan, on Allen Street just off Delancey. It has three tables, two of which accommodate four people and one that accommodates two, under which there is a mysterious pipe that protrudes from the floor and abruptly terminates at ankle level.

Now, you can't just go to Fried Dumpling and expect to be fed. You have to work for your meal, because every customer at Fried Dumpling is as alone as Robinson Crusoe. It's you versus the other customers, and you versus the restaurant. Lose your concentration for a split second, and you're at the back of the line.

An order of pan-fried dumplings—among the best available in New York, with thin, crispy skins and a scallion-laced ground-pork filling—costs a dollar and includes five dumplings. This presents a nomenclature problem, because if you say you want five dumplings, they ask if you want five dumplings or five orders of dumplings. If, however, you say you want one order of dumplings, they scowl and explain that there is a five-dumpling minimum.

You douse the dumplings in sweetened soy sauce and Sriracha hot Thai-style pepper sauce (or at least some sort of hot sauce, placed in a Sriracha plastic squeeze bottle). One order makes a nice snack, two a fine lunch, and three a filling dinner. Only the heavy hitters go for four.

There do appear to be other items on the menu (a sign posted above the counter), but I don't believe even half of them have ever actually emerged from the kitchen. Most of the time, if you try to order something else, you're told "Fried dumpling, five for a dollar, fried dumpling," a behavior pattern reminiscent of John Belushi's greasy-spoon chef from *Saturday Night Live*: "Cheeseburger, cheeseburger, cheeseburger; no Coke—Pepsi."

Once you have your food, the fight for tables begins, and any empty seat is fair game. I have shared my table with many a stranger, but only once had a conversation—with a guy who for no reason assumed I had a good working knowledge of Windows NT. In better weather, you can also eat in the nearby park.

Uncooked dumplings are also available to go, frozen, at $5 for thirty pieces. They're great for parties, and it's 20 percent less expensive than eating them at the restaurant. But of course, when you dine at Fried Dumpling, you're paying for the ambience.

INTERMEDIATE: DIM SUM SURVIVAL GUIDE

While the dim sum brunch is gaining popularity in North America, many people find it a confusing and intimidating experience. That's because they don't know how to behave—or, rather, not behave—at a dim sum brunch.

Dim sum, Cantonese for "touch the heart" but used colloquially to mean "morsel," refers to a variety of little snack-like items eaten for a late morning meal. Many Chinese restaurants, even in areas without significant Asian populations, serve dim sum brunch on weekends. The most common setup involves rolling metal carts stacked high with individual steamers. The servers roll the carts around and you get whatever you want off the cart. For each item you take, the server generally stamps, punches, or checks off the relevant information on your bill (which remains on the table throughout the meal). In some old-school dim sum places, they instead count the plates left on the table at the end of the meal (different colors, sizes, and shapes of plates might correspond to $3 items, $4 items, and so on).

Here are ten rules for dim sum survival.

Get in the Mind-set

The dim sum brunch is one of the restaurant world's purest exercises in social Darwinism. The meek etiquette of the Western world is hopelessly overmatched in the dim sum ecosystem. In order to thrive under the dim sum law of the jungle, you need to get in the mind-set of people from a country with a billion inhabitants. It's eat or let your food be eaten by someone else.

Observe the Rhythms

You need to get in touch with the life cycle of the dim sum brunch, just as a hunter in the primordial jungle needs to know when his prey is out and about. At most dim sum restaurants, the ideal time to be there is within an hour of opening. As the day wears on, the selection thins out, the kitchen starts to run ragged, and, near closing time, the ratio of dregs to good stuff becomes unacceptable.

Have Patience

Don't fill up on whatever junk comes your way first. You need to be intelligent about your selection. Especially if you know the restaurant and know what's good, there's no excuse for eating what's bad. If you need to pass the time, go ahead and reference the scene in *Working Girl* when Melanie Griffith wheels around a steaming dim sum cart at Sigourney Weaver's party; then if you get desperate, mention that dim sum dates back to teahouses in China during the Sung Dynasty (A.D. 960–1280).

Be Decisive

If you see something great on a cart, bear in mind that you may very well never see it again. So take it. Quickly. Before the cart escapes. And take as many of it as you think you'll want. This requirement can come in conflict with the virtue of patience. It's a delicate balancing act.

Be Flexible

The food you want may not come in the order you want it. Too bad. The moment you decided to go out for dim sum, you gave up the right to get your food custom-sequenced. Take the good stuff when it arrives. Period.

Be Pushy

To get the most out of a dim sum experience, you need to be pushy. Very pushy. If you see a cart or tray across the room and you're curious about it, get up and walk right over. Ask questions. Make demands. If you don't see something you want, ask for it—the kitchen can probably produce it within a few minutes.

Gamble

Dim sum items are cheap. Don't worry about getting something you don't like—the cost of failure is only a few dollars. If you're curious, try it. If it's not to your liking, someone else at your table might like it, and if nobody likes it you can just set it aside and chalk it up to experience.

Get It While It's Hot

Figure out where the carts are coming from—usually there are swinging kitchen doors somewhere—and get to them on their first pass around the dining room. One of the best ways to do this, if you can control the situation, is to be seated near the kitchen. Under no circumstances should you be taking food from nearly empty carts that have been cruising around for half an hour. And you definitely don't want to take the limpid remainders the servers sometimes bring around on hand-carried trays. Let some other sucker eat that stuff. You want to get the hottest, freshest, best food the moment it emerges from the kitchen.

Be a Leader

Success in dim sum starts long before you enter the restaurant. You should organize the largest possible group so you get to try the most items. Before you eat, you should brief the group on good dim sum strategy, so you don't have some Nervous Nellie breaking ranks and bringing the team down. And at the restaurant, you should take responsibility for your flock, because many of them won't pay enough attention to feed themselves well. Luckily, they have you.

Know What's What

The following is a brief glossary of the dim sum items that tend to be the best at Chinese restaurants in North America. Of course, the selection will vary by restaurant, and this list is just the tip of the iceberg—there are hundreds of variants. If you can use the Chinese lingo, you may increase your stock a bit in the eyes of the waitstaff.

Har gow (steamed shrimp dumplings): chunks of shrimp in a translucent wheat-starch wrapper; usually a good test of a dim sum kitchen's skills. Also: *jai gow* (steamed vegetable dumplings).

Char siu bau (steamed pork buns): sweet Cantonese roast pork and onions in a white, fluffy, steamed wheat-flour bun; there's also a baked variant that's golden brown and shiny.

Chee cheong fun (steamed wide rice-noodle rolls): these look like miniature glossy burritos and can be filled with shrimp, mushrooms, or most anything else.

No mai gai (lotus leaf rice): glutinous rice wrapped in a leaf (you don't eat the leaf) and steamed; in with the rice are many little treasures, usually at least egg, mushrooms, water chestnuts, and pork.

Dan ta (egg custard tart): this is a dessert item with a flaky crust and a yellow custard filling. It looks like an individual Western-style tart; indeed they are probably an adaptation of British tarts brought to Hong Kong in the 1940s.

ADVANCED: BREAKING THE MOLD

In most of North America, the average Chinese restaurant will have a very large menu incorporating dishes from the

NEW GREEN BABY

New Green Bo has long been a favorite local Chinese restaurant, but not because of the service. My wife and I had been going there once or twice a month for almost the duration of our marriage, and while the food was always excellent, nobody ever acknowledged that we'd been there before. It was like *Groundhog Day*, the restaurant edition: we remembered eating there, but to the waitstaff it all seemed new each time.

A few years into our relationship with New Green Bo, we received a glimmer of acknowledgment. A group of friends from Canada came to town, and I took them to New Green Bo, which they insist to this day on calling "The New Green Bow." The servers at New Green Bo are impatient. You're expected to make your decisions quickly, order everything at once, eat, and get out. This bunch of Canadians, unfamiliar with Shanghainese cuisine, was driving them crazy with hesitation and questions. Finally, the manager met my eyes and gave me a look of desperation. "Can't you take control of this situation? You come here all the time," she communicated to me telepathically. I took charge, placed the order, and averted disaster. On the way out, the manager actually said "Thank you!"

The next week, though, it was back to being ignored.

Now, I'm pretty good at getting friendly with people who work in restaurants. I may be the world's leading expert on the subject, or perhaps the only expert, since I've written a book on it and nobody else has. But I was never, ever able to make headway with the New Green Bo staff.

Why keep going there, then? Because it's the best Shanghainese restaurant outside of Shanghai, and it's cheap. No matter how much you order—and I order a lot—you can't spend more than about $36 on dinner, and you can't possibly finish all that food. Any time I go to another Chinese restaurant and order the same things I get at New Green Bo, I'm disappointed. So, like many people, I put up with New Green Bo's foibles because it offers such good food and such great value.

Then one day we went into New Green Bo with our newborn baby boy, PJ, and everything changed. The entire staff gathered around. They made faces. They made noises. They offered cookies. Every time a dish got delivered to our table, our server would stop to admire the baby. They even refilled our water glasses diligently throughout the meal.

Now, whenever we go to New Green Bo, we're greeted with big smiles and warm salutations. When PJ was about sixteen months old, we got a fortune cookie with a "Learn Chinese" phrase on the back. It said "Hai-Zu=Children." I read it aloud, and PJ said "Hai-Zu!" It was one of his first words. The applause from the staff was thunderous.

Another night, when we were lucky enough to have the babysitting services of my mother, we showed up at New Green Bo without the baby. "Where is baby?" we were challenged with suspicion. We explained that my mother was babysitting. The manager's scowling verdict: "Next time, bring baby."

We will.

Chinese-American repertoire as well as various regional Chinese dishes, and perhaps Southeast Asian, Korean, and Japanese dishes too. In areas with large Asian populations, however, specialization is likely to occur. Although there are countless regional cuisines of China, two styles of restaurants in particular have become popular in North America lately: Sichuan and Shanghai.

At both of these types of restaurants, it pays to know a few of the key dishes. At the same time, your most effective strategy will always be to extract information from the waiters. Here are eight global strategy tips that apply to all advanced Chinese-restaurant dining, whether the restaurant specializes in Sichuan, Shanghai, Hunan, Cantonese seafood, or Fuzhou cuisine.

Point and Stare

My e-mail in-box is full of testimonials from people complaining that they went to a Chinese restaurant and saw a table of Chinese people eating dishes they couldn't identify or find on the menu. The simplest way to navigate that problem is to point at the dishes and ask what they are. It's most polite to ask the restaurant's staff, but it's also expedient to walk over to the table and say, "Excuse me, I'm terribly sorry to interrupt your meal, but do you think you could tell me what you're eating?" People who are proud of their cultural heritage will most likely be thrilled at the opportunity to share their knowledge. In one case, after striking up such a conversation with a Chinese family, the oldest daughter (who was also, it turned out, a food-magazine editor) walked over with me to the owner of the restaurant and helped me negotiate an order that resulted in one of the best Chinese meals I've ever had.

Start at the Top

When I walk into an unfamiliar Chinese restaurant, the first thing I do is try to identify the top-ranking person in the room. Usually it's the guy in the nicest suit. This is the person who's likely to speak the best English and have the greatest ability to help you.

Take Responsibility

The main reason Chinese restaurants don't offer the best, most interesting Chinese dishes to their mainstream customers is that they think those customers won't like or want to pay for the best stuff. Before you can reach across the cultural divide and get access to the best dishes, then, you need to relieve the restaurant of responsibility. If you state loudly and clearly that you're an adventurous eater, that you're willing to pay for the special dishes, and that you won't hold the restaurant responsible if you don't like the taste of an unusual dish, you'll bring yourself several steps closer to being treated like a Chinese insider.

Be Adventurous, and Know Your Limits

There's no point in going through the ritual of demanding "the real stuff" if you're not going to like it. So it's best to know your limits when you order. Are you able to handle fish with bones in it? Nonmainstream parts of animals (pig ear)? A ton of hot chilies (I once got a dish of "chicken with chilies" that had more chilies than chicken)? If not, admit your limits so you can order what you'll actually enjoy.

Assemble a Large Group

The Western model of meal service at modern restaurants (called "service à la Russe" in technical terms) is for each dish to be plated individually: one person orders steak, and the steak is placed in front of that person; another person orders chicken, and gets chicken. Chinese meal service (and also service in many other types of Asian restaurants, though usually not Japanese) proceeds family-style: platters and bowls are placed in the middle of the table and everybody shares. People who dine in conventional Western restaurants know that the more people you eat with, the worse the meal gets: if you have a table of eight, the service will be slow because the kitchen can be overwhelmed by processing all those orders simultaneously. But in Chinese restaurants it's the opposite: the more people you have with you, the better your meal will be because you get to sample more dishes from a large selection presented family-style.

Plan Ahead

One of the best ways to take a large group to a Chinese restaurant (and this strategy works at other types of Asian restaurants as well) is to walk into the restaurant a couple of days before the meal, present yourself to the proprietor or head manager, and say, for example, "Ten of us are coming on Wednesday night at seven P.M., and we'd like to arrange a meal for three hundred and fifty dollars total. What would you suggest for a menu?" State your preferences and your level of adventurousness, and see what the restaurant proposes. Then you can have some back-and-forth—"Let's try to get a duck dish in there"—and eventually settle on a menu. And you can be sure that when your group shows up for the meal, you'll be taken seriously.

Read Everything

Before you're seated, be sure to ask for every menu, whether it's in English or Chinese. You should be able to eyeball the stacks of different menus sitting behind the hostess stand or somewhere else near the front of the restaurant. Don't settle for less than every menu. If there are menus printed only in Chinese, point to random items and ask what they are, and also ask what the best items on that page are. If there are lists of specials on the wall written only in Chinese, again ask for a translation. If you want to dine like an insider, you need to do whatever it takes to get the information.

Go with Chinese Friends

No amount of strategizing or book-learning is a substitute for in-person guidance from a friend of Chinese ancestry. Not all descendants of Chinese immigrants know or care about Chinese food. But if you show up at a Chinese restaurant with even one Chinese person at your table, and that person has some food knowledge and perhaps even Chinese-language skills, you can often break through a lot of resistance. Of course, in order to do this, you need to have Chinese friends—or you need to make some.

SICHUAN AND SHANGHAI RESTAURANTS are the two specialty restaurants you're most likely to find in cities and suburbs with large Chinese populations. It's not possible to describe every dish you might encounter at one of these restaurants, but the ones described below will get you started. Most of these restaurants will offer the standard Westernized Chinese-menu items as well, so be sure to look for the house specialties further along into the menu.

Sichuan

If I had to pick a favorite Chinese cuisine, it would be Sichuan. The most notable aspect of Sichuan cuisine is that it uses hot chilies as well as Sichuan peppercorns. Sichuan peppercorns—which at times have been illegal to import to the United States due to fears of a citrus canker that, if spread, could threaten crops—are not really peppercorns at all but rather small buds that cause an unusual tingling on the tongue (the Chinese call this *mala,* or "numbing spiciness"). The word "Sichuan" (or "Szechuan") in a restaurant's name, however, doesn't necessarily mean that it's a restaurant serving real Sichuan food. Words like "Sichuan," "Hunan," and "Mandarin" are bandied about in Chinese-restaurant names, often with seeming randomness. Meanwhile, one of my favorite Sichuan restaurants doesn't even have the word "Sichuan" in its name: it's called Wu Liang Ye, named for a kind of Chinese liquor.

The following are five of my favorite Sichuan dishes.

Dan dan noodles. These are cold spaghetti-thickness noodles with a spicy, tongue-numbing sauce made from both hot chilies and Sichuan peppercorns, with peanuts, sesame, and garlic, usually garnished with shredded cucumber. Take a break after you eat them, because you may not be able to taste anything else for a few minutes. There's also a cold-chicken equivalent called *bon bon chicken* made with the same sauce, and when that sauce is poured over small steamed meat dumplings, the dish is called *suan la chow show*. Unfortunately, the naming conventions for these dishes are not entirely standardized, so you might see *dan dan* written as *tan tan*, *bon bon* written as *bong bong*, or *suan la chow show* described as something like "Sichuan spicy wontons."

Kung pao chicken. A dish called *kung pao chicken* is often found on standard Westernized Chinese-restaurant menus, and in those cases it's a simple dish of diced chicken and peanuts in a brown sauce. Real Sichuan kung pao chicken, however, is loaded with hot chilies and Sichuan peppercorns, and is a fiery but delicate dish worth seeking out. At one restaurant I frequent, Grand Sichuan International Midtown, there's even the option to have the dish made with freshly killed chicken (described on the menu as "not long time refrigerated"). I love the dish so much that I've considered plans to build a kung pao chicken pipeline from Grand Sichuan International Midtown to my home that would terminate in a spigot out of which steaming hot kung pao chicken would pour into a tin cup at any hour of the day or night.

Twice-cooked pork. Twice-cooked pork is first simmered in water seasoned with ginger and salt, then sliced and fried in a wok with cabbage and peppers. The trick with ordering twice-cooked pork is that, to get the best version, you have to ask for it fatty. At most real Sichuan restaurants you can simply say, "Fatty, like Chinese people like it." Otherwise, the kitchen will make it for you with lean slices of pork that are not all that interesting. But if you get it fatty, the slices are like a cross between ribs and bacon.

Ma po tofu. Though it sounds like it might be a vegetarian dish, ma po tofu is actually made with ground meat and little cubes of tofu in a Sichuan peppercorn–enhanced bean sauce. It's my favorite tofu dish. This is another dish, however, that's not worth getting at a mainstream Chinese restaurant, where it's often prepared without meat, Sichuan peppercorns, or much skill and the sauce is gloppy and sweet.

Tea-smoked duck. The duck is marinated in tea and spices, and then smoked in a sealed wok over camphor-wood chips. Every chef I've spoken to has a slightly different take on how to make tea-smoked duck, but the camphor-smoked taste is the unifying theme. If a restaurant does this dish well, it can be one of the best examples of Sichuan cuisine. And, unlike many Sichuan dishes, it's barely spicy, so when you plan a Sichuan meal it can add balance.

Shanghai

Shanghai is not a culinary region but is, rather, a port city famous for being home to many of China's best restaurants. Shanghai cuisine is highly refined, urban, and sophisticated. Unlike Sichuan cuisine, most Shanghai dishes are not spicy. Much of Shanghai cuisine draws from the nearby coastal provinces of Jiangsu and Zhejiang, though there are influences from all over China and, because Shanghai has long been a maritime trading center, from around the world. For starch, Shanghai cuisine tends to emphasize breads and noodles over rice. I've found that Europeans, in particular, appreciate Shanghai cuisine because it's subtle and because many dishes demonstrate a level of restraint reminiscent of what you'd find in French or Italian kitchens.

Here are a few of my favorite Shanghai dishes.

Xiao lung bao. Often called "soup dumplings" or "juicy buns," xiao lung bao (sometimes written "xiaolongbao") are beggar's purse–shaped steamed dumplings filled with meat (usually a combination of pork and crabmeat, or just pork) and, miraculously, soup. It's a shame to reveal how they get the soup into the dumplings (kind of like a magician revealing his secrets), but after you make everybody at the table guess, you can disclose the method: the chef makes a heavily reduced soup stock that when refrigerated firms up like Jell-O. A dollop of this cold, gelatinous stock is placed in each dumpling along with the meat filling. When the dumplings are steamed, the gelatin liquefies. To eat xiao lung bao, which are served in a bamboo steamer, stick your spoon right into the steamer next to a dumpling, then grab the tip of the beggar's purse (either with tongs or with your fingers) and quickly transfer it to the spoon. (Don't try to pick up a soup dumpling with chopsticks or a fork—you'll get soup everywhere.) Then bring the spoon to your mouth and bite off a little corner of the dumpling, tilting it so that the soup won't all run out. You can now suck the soup out of the dumpling. Then add a little of the black vinegar and ginger sauce that comes on the side—just a few drops—and finish eating the dumpling. Be sure to relay all this advice to your dining companions before they eat any xiao lung bao, in order to preempt disaster. Order more xiao lung bao than you think you'll need, because everybody loves them.

Lion's-head meatballs. No, they're not made from lions, or heads. The name comes from the size of the meatballs, which are quite large—sometimes three inches in diameter. These pork meatballs are stewed slowly with cabbage, and it's said that the cabbage looks like a lion's mane. Well-made lion's-head meatballs can give any Italian or Swedish meatballs a real run for their money.

Red-cooked pork. Red cooking, which involves long simmering in a soy-based broth with sugar and star anise, is one of the signatures of Shanghai cuisine (Shanghai is known for the finest soy sauce in China). Red-cooked meat is called *hong shao rou*. My favorite red-cooked dish is red-cooked pork belly. Pork belly is essentially fresh, uncured, unsliced bacon. When red cooked, the pork belly acquires deep flavors and the meat is naturally braised by the fatty layer on top. Red-cooked pork sometimes comes with little sesame-studded buns on the side, which are useful vehicles for conveying the pork to your mouth.

Yellow fish. These little fingers of fried white-fleshed fish (it can be made with any of a number of types of fish) are enhanced by seaweed in the batter. They're utterly addictive, so much so that one restaurant's version (a place called Goody's) inspired the former *New York Times* restaurant reviewer Ruth Reichl to write: "It tastes like deep-fried sushi, and it is the most delicious fried fish I have ever eaten."

Rice cakes. Fear not, Shanghai rice cakes have nothing to do with the puffed-rice snacks sold in Western health-food stores. Rather, they're a type of noodle made from glutinous rice. The rice is manufactured into the shape of a log, and then the log is sliced into disks, which are then cooked like noodles (boiled, then stir-fried). You can get rice cakes with chicken, pork, mushrooms, vegetables—basically all the permutations you'd find for lo mein or fried rice in a standard Westernized Chinese restaurant. Rice cakes have a unique, wonderful, chewy texture and are a good light dish to balance the richness of much of Shanghai cuisine.

CHICKEN POWDER AND ORANGE PEEL BEEF: A CHAT WITH BETTY XIE

Betty Xie is the editor in chief of *Chinese Restaurant News* magazine, a monthly publication launched in July 1995 and printed in Chinese (it's also online at www.c-r-n.com). It is the must-read information source for Chinese restaurateurs, tracking industry news and trends for the more than 43,000 Chinese restaurants in the United States. Betty was kind enough to spend some time answering my questions about the Chinese-restaurant business.

STEVEN: "I've noticed that more and more often, Chinese restaurants are serving other Asian cuisines in addition to Chinese food. In particular, sushi and Thai food. Do you have any statistics about this trend? Is there a reason restaurateurs are giving you for the decision to serve these other kinds of food?"

BETTY: "In recent years, we've heard a lot about how many Chinese restaurants are shabby and outdated, and how Chinese food is oily, salty, and cheap. This bad reputation, which to some degree can be very true, has deeply hurt the Chinese restaurant industry. There has been nearly a 50 percent increase in Chinese restaurants since the late 1990s (there were under 30,000 Chinese restaurants in 1996 and more than 43,000 in 2006, according to our own database), and many of these new restaurants are operated by new immigrant families who work very hard. So a lot of Chinese restaurants are competing with themselves solely on price point, and they are ultimately left with no margin to improve. At the same time, Japanese and Thai cuisines are getting more and more popular among mainstream consumers. It could be that because of this, many well-established Chinese restaurants have had to expand their menus and add more Asian dishes, just to be more appealing to diners."

STEVEN: "It seems that many Chinese restaurants have the same or similar menus. Is there a company somewhere that provides a Chinese restaurant starter kit that includes a standard menu? If not, do you know how this menu developed and is distributed?"

BETTY: "No, not likely. The 'standard menu' scenario is an interesting phenomenon even to Chinese people themselves. Mostly, chefs or staff would open a new restaurant of their own after working a few years at a Chinese restaurant and keep the same menu. Another guess is that Chinese restaurant people would not want to risk their investments by changing the menu and selling dishes that Americans would not eat. The safe way to go is to copy someone else's menu. The menus are similar, but the dishes by no means get to a standard. It could read the same 'Chow Mein' on the menus, but the noodles can vary from thin to thick to crispy ones from restaurant to restaurant. The color of shrimp fried rice in the East Coast can be dark, while in San Francisco it can be white."

STEVEN: "Do you have any information about what percentage of Chinese restaurants are family-owned and what percentage are part of chains?"

BETTY: "We have some estimates. Based on CRN's database, 80 percent–plus are family-owned, 15 percent–plus are part of small regional chains run by families, relatives, or partnerships (not franchised). We see more of these regional chains that own three to ten locations. Some have twenty to thirty shops. Big chains like Panda Express, P.F. Chang's, Manchu Wok, Hy-Vee Chinese Express, Leeann Chin, Mark Pi's, et cetera, take up less than 5 percent of the segment."

STEVEN: "And do you know what percentage are buffets? Also, what's the total number of Chinese restaurants in America?"

BETTY: "The total number of Chinese restaurants in the U.S. is 43,139, per our database in January of 2007. Chinese buffets are definitely on the rise. The first Chinese buffets started in Canada, and then they came to New York. The fastest-growing area for buffets was in Texas in the late 1990s since the rent was cheap there. One of our advertisers who sells buffet tables actually moved the entire company from New York to Texas in 1999 because so many of their customers came from Texas. We don't have an exact percentage of buffets, but a safe estimate would be around 10 percent."

STEVEN: "Do you have any information about the declining use of MSG in Chinese restaurants? It seems more and more menus say 'no MSG.' Are there any statistics about this?"

BETTY: "Definitely the trend of 'no MSG' is continuing. In 1998 we had three or four companies that advertised their MSG products in *Chinese Restaurant News*. Now all of those companies seem to have vanished. Chicken powder replaces MSG. One Japanese company that made big profits on MSG now faces a real crisis as how to switch their products to more healthy options."

STEVEN: "Do you have a list of the most-ordered dishes in Chinese restaurants in America?"

BETTY: "Eggrolls, pot stickers (dumplings), wonton soup, barbecue pork, hot-and-sour soup, sweet-and-sour pork, beef with broccoli, kung pao chicken, moo shu pork, Mongolian beef, cashew chicken, orange-peel beef, General Tso's chicken, lemon chicken, sesame chicken (most sweet, sour, spicy taste—profiled dishes sell well), fried rice. Recently, Beijing duck, shu mai, har gow (a type of Chinese dim sum), char siu bao (barbecue pork—stuffed steamed buns), lettuce wrap with shredded chicken, ma po tofu, summer roll."

Chinese Food and Health: Junk science and junk food

Two sets of health concerns have besieged Chinese restaurants in recent decades: first, concerns about salt and fat; second, concerns about MSG. Both sets of concerns are unfounded.

CHINESE FOOD VERSUS THE BIG MAC

Back in 1993, and again in 2007, the Center for Science in the Public Interest (CSPI) generated scores of media reports claiming that Chinese food is unhealthy. In the September 1993 *Nutrition Action Health Letter*, an article titled "Chinese Food: A Wok on the Wild Side" made three comparisons that have remained in the public consciousness to this day:

- An order of kung pao chicken with almost as much fat as four Quarter Pounders
- An order of moo shu pork with more than twice the cholesterol of an Egg McMuffin
- An order of house lo mein with as much salt as a whole Pizza Hut Cheese Pizza

The 1993 article begins, provocatively, "According to a recent report by the Food Marketing Institute and Prevention Magazine, 52 percent of all Americans say that Chinese food is 'more healthful' than their usual diet. If only they knew." It then goes on to debunk this alleged myth with analyses of fifteen dishes, concluding that "the average Chinese dinner we looked at contains more sodium than you should eat in an entire day. It also has 70 percent of a day's fat, 80 percent of a day's cholesterol, and almost half a day's saturated fat."

Then, in 2007, the CSPI returned to the well and published "Wok Carefully: CSPI Takes a (Second) Look at Chinese Restaurant Food." It begins, "Popular Chinese restaurant meals can contain an entire day's worth of sodium and some contain two days' worth." In both 1993 and 2007, the CSPI pieces were not unequivocally negative. They offered advice for reducing sodium, saturated fat, and cholesterol through better ordering and portion control. But these parts weren't what made headlines like:

- "Chinese restaurant food unhealthy, study says: Menus loaded with sodium, saturated fat and calories—even the veggies" (MSNBC)
- "Study: Chinese Restaurant Food Unhealthy: Typical Chinese Restaurant Menu Is a Sea of Nutritional No-Nos, According to Consumer Group" (USA Today)

But is Chinese food unhealthy? There are several fallacies underlying the CSPI's conclusions.

The so-called study (it's really just a test of the nutritional content of a few dishes, and some of that information was gathered from unreliable sources on the Internet rather than the more legitimate method of laboratory analysis) makes the assumption that an entire take-out order of kung pao chicken equals one dinner for one person. Yet there is no basis for this assumption. Rather, it is common for a family to order several dishes and share them—and to have leftovers. As Albert Chang, owner of Grant Place restaurant in San Francisco, told Asian Week magazine in reaction to the CSPI's 2007 report, "Chinese food is usually eaten family style, so it is not accurate to say the sodium count for one dish is too much for one person."

The CSPI also doesn't offer any information about what dishes people actually order in a typical Chinese meal. If a family of four orders three or four dishes, are they all going to be from the "bad" list, or will some be vegetables, shrimp, and other dishes that, along with steamed white rice, balance some of the heavier dishes? Somebody is ordering those vegetables; otherwise they wouldn't be on the menu.

Perhaps the most glaring fallacy, especially in the 2007 report, is the emphasis on the evils of sodium. It's astounding that the CSPI, as well as many other groups that should know better, is still railing against salt as if there has been no progress in medical knowledge since the 1970s. At this point, the health claims against salt have been so thoroughly debunked that it's hard to imagine any research-based organization being unaware that the salt-hypertension connection is a myth. Given current scientific knowledge, the only thing that can be said with certainty about salt and hypertension is that a percentage of the population may possibly be "salt sensitive." However, for healthy individuals with normally functioning kidneys, there's no reason to be concerned about salt. Putting the nation on a sodium-restricted diet makes as much sense as treating the entire population for a condition that affects only people with blue eyes. Worse, by steering people away from foods solely on the basis of salt content, the CSPI is discouraging the ordering of lower-fat items, like soups.

The comparisons to McDonald's and Pizza Hut are

particularly disingenuous. Chinese-restaurant menus are huge and they emphasize choice. No American who has turned on a television or radio, read a newspaper, or surfed the Web could be unaware that steamed broccoli has fewer calories per ounce than deep-fried pork. If people want to order healthful, wholesome, delicious meals at Chinese restaurants, it's the easiest thing in the world to do. Western fast-food restaurants, on the other hand, offer only token options for the health-conscious, and they're almost never good (or healthful).

But the most troublesome aspect of the CSPI's strategy is that it represents an attack on an entire culture. Despite some backpedaling in the 2007 report ("Many Chinese entrées are loaded with healthy vegetables and lean shrimp or chicken"), statements like "When it comes to sodium, there's no real safe harbor on the Chinese restaurant menu" are irresponsible generalizations. Andrew Poon of San Francisco's Far East Café told *Asian Week,* "There's so many different kinds and types of Chinese food, its unfair to say all Chinese food is salty." It's such an obvious answer to such a heavy-handed generalization, yet in fourteen years it never occurred to the CSPI to take a more nuanced approach. Chinese food has been under attack since the day the first Chinese restaurants opened on our shores. It's time for a change.

MSG: SYNDROME OR PSYCHOSIS?

In early 1968, a Cantonese doctor named Robert Kwok was doing his residency at a hospital in Silver Spring, Maryland. Dr. Kwok wrote a letter to the *New England Journal of Medicine* alleging that whenever he ate Chinese-American food, he experienced a numbness in his neck, back, and arms lasting for about two hours after the meal. A month later, the *New England Journal of Medicine* published ten other letters from people claiming to have observed the same phenomenon. The search for the cause of "Chinese Restaurant Syndrome" was on.

At first there were several theories, with perhaps the prime suspect being salt. In a May 1968 article in the *New York Times,* the theory was described thus: "The high salt content of the Chinese food may produce a temporary excess of sodium in the blood that reduces the potassium levels of the body. This, in turn, can cause a numbness of the muscles, generalized weakness and throbbing." Other candidates were soy sauce, Chinese cooking wine, and the flavoring agent monosodium glutamate (MSG).

By the 1970s, however, MSG had pulled ahead of the field. Tried and convicted in the court of public opinion—though not in the court of science—the conventional wisdom became that MSG causes Chinese Restaurant Syndrome. In the United States to this day, it is a widely held belief that MSG is responsible for a variety of ills.

But there are a number of problems with this theory.

Since the early twentieth century, MSG has been used widely in Asian foods. Though associated with Chinese food in the public consciousness, MSG was discovered by Prof. Kidunae Ikeda, a physicist at Tokyo Imperial University, after he learned that his wife (not to mention just about every cook in Japan) seasoned the family's soup with *kombu,* a type of seaweed. He observed that the flavor it imparted to the soup was not one of the four tastes—sweet, sour, salty, bitter—commonly held to be the complete set of tastes. Instead, he wrote, "There is a taste which is common to asparagus, tomatoes, cheese and meat but which is not one of the four well-known tastes." He named the taste umami, which depending on who you ask is Japanese for "savory" or "deliciousness."

Chemical analysis revealed that the compound $C_5H_9NO_4$, or glutamic acid, was responsible for the flavor-enhancing properties of kombu. This compound, when subjected to the heat of cooking, breaks down and becomes glutamate. Professor Ikeda then sought to synthesize and stabilize glutamic acid, and was able to do so by mixing it with salt and water to form monosodium glutamate, or MSG. He patented the process and started marketing MSG as Ajinomoto. By the time of his death in 1936, MSG was in widespread use all over Asia. MSG made the jump to North America mostly after World War II.

At this point, MSG has been around for so long—longer than fettuccine Alfredo, coq au vin, or Caesar salad—that it is properly classified as a traditional food of Asia. In restaurant and home kitchens across Asia, it is commonplace to find "Gourmet Powder" in use (in North America it's called Accent). This state of affairs prompted the food writer Jeffrey Steingarten to ask, "If MSG is so bad for you, why doesn't everyone in Asia have a headache?" This question remains unanswered.

In addition, the naturally occurring version of MSG, glutamate, is found in many foods in quantities that if MSG really causes Chinese Restaurant Syndrome should cause the syndrome in most Americans every day—whether they eat Chinese food or not. Examples of glutamate-rich foods range from Parmesan cheese and tomatoes to cured meats and even mother's milk. Indeed, our bodies produce about forty grams of it a day. Some have argued that the commercial form of MSG contains impurities and chemical agents that trigger different reactions than naturally occurring glutamate, but scientific studies have not supported this contention.

MSG is used liberally, across the food supply, in countless non-Asian foods. If you pull almost any packaged food off the shelf in an American supermarket, you will see that it lists monosodium glutamate as an ingredient, or if it doesn't, it lists one of the many ingredients that contain glutamate, such as calcium caseinate, yeast extract, hydrolyzed protein, and hydrolyzed corn gluten. (Food companies use this creative labeling to avoid the negative associations with MSG.)

Moreover, scientific studies have demonstrated, time and again, that MSG is harmless to humans. Though various holistic nutritionists and other pseudoscientists have made a cottage industry of MSG scaremongering, mainstream science has never supported such a link. The United States Food and Drug Administration has been studying MSG since the 1950s and has never found any evidence to indicate that it causes harm.

So if MSG is not the culprit, what explains Chinese Restaurant Syndrome?

Most likely, the answer is that there is no one explanation. As researchers at the University of Western Sydney concluded in 1993, "Chinese restaurant syndrome is an anecdote applied to a variety of postprandial illnesses; rigorous and realistic scientific evidence linking the syndrome to MSG could not be found."

Unfamiliar or different foods, including foods consumed regularly but occasionally, can cause a variety of reactions. Those who rarely eat beans often experience flatulence when they do, whereas people who eat beans all the time are less likely to react that way. Travelers' diarrhea is often blamed on parasites, but is actually most often caused by the way people eat on vacation: unusual foods and alcohol, and lots of both, combined with long days on the beach followed by long nights of partying can cause gastrointestinal distress as sure as any microorganism. It is certainly possible that those who think they're experiencing Chinese Restaurant Syndrome are simply reacting to a change in diet. This would help explain why the billion-plus people in China, where MSG is widely used, don't appear to have Chinese Restaurant Syndrome.

FAREWELL, HUNAN K

Hunan K was our neighborhood Chinese restaurant, though to call it a restaurant is an exaggeration. You've seen this sort of place: a storefront the width of a locksmith's shop; a couple of rarely used tables wedged awkwardly into the vestibule; a series of surreal photographs of Chinese-American dishes posted above the counter; and three generations of a family working hard, twelve or more hours a day, in the exposed kitchen.

Hunan K was not a good Chinese restaurant, or even a mediocre Chinese restaurant. It was a bad Chinese restaurant, though I don't mean that in a bad way. Having grown up with bad Chinese food, I find that certain perverse examples of it—egg foo yung smothered in gelatinous brown gravy; Day-Glo-red sweet-and-sour chicken—bring me comfort. I'm gratified that Shanghai, Fuzhou, and other regional Chinese cuisines are now expressing themselves in America, but I'd be sorry to see the bad-Chinese-restaurant breed die out.

Hunan K opened almost on the same day that we moved to Manhattan's Carnegie Hill, though any resident of Carnegie Hill would be quick to point out that Hunan K, being on Third Avenue, is not in the neighborhood. We visited Hunan K, perhaps on opening day, or at least thereabouts, and dismissed it as generic and unfortunate.

Hunan K, it turns out, did not deserve such premature dismissal. Over time, we made enemies with each of the six or seven other bad Chinese restaurants nearby. At some point, each would commit an unthinkable transgression in cuisine or service, and we would cross it off our list. Eventually, Hunan K was the last bad Chinese restaurant standing. So we returned (I returned, actually, because I am the designated take-out schlepper).

Hunan K, it became apparent, was a deeper operation than I had originally assumed. Because while the emphasis was on bad Chinese food, all the makings of good Chinese food were present as well. The primary cook had trained at one or another impressive-sounding Asian hotel. Right next to the gigantic cans of goopy industrial sauces were all the fresh vegetables and meats one would need to create a wedding banquet. The bad-Chinese-food orientation was purely an expression of supply and demand. As I became a regular customer, I started making special requests. These requests were fulfilled with aplomb, and further suggestions were proffered. Eventually, good Chinese food emerged from Hunan K, although

I confess my typical order juxtaposed the good and the bad.

Hunan K was accommodating in the extreme. There were several dishes the chef and I concocted together to satisfy my wife's mostly vegetarian leanings, my favorite being mushroom and cabbage soup (pronounced "musroomcabbasoop"). Amazingly, even when the head cook was not present (he took a day off every month or so), it was possible to get musroomcabbasoop from the auxiliary cooks—everybody knew all my special orders. The price arrived at for a quart of this elixir was an arbitrary $2.60, which never changed over the years.

Hunan K delivered via bicycle, of course, but I preferred to visit the restaurant and witness the ballet in the kitchen. The efficiency and economy of movement of this family, as the members cooked multiple large and small take-out orders with flawless coordination, were preternatural. I did on occasion have food delivered, though, and the delivery guy always came up the stairs laughing. "Ha ha ha ha, hello how are you sir. Ha ha ha ha ha. Ten ninety five. Ha ha ha ha ha. Thank you very much have nice day. Ha ha ha ha ha." We came to refer to him as "the guy with the maniac laugh." Once I was walking on Park Avenue and the guy with the maniac laugh rode past me on his bicycle. As soon as I registered in his consciousness, he slammed on his brakes. "Ha ha ha ha ha. Hello sir! Ha ha ha ha." And then he observed with existential flair, "You on the street! Ha ha ha ha ha."

A couple of years ago, Hunan K closed its doors forever. I headed there one night to obtain musroomcabbasoop, exact change for two orders in my pocket. But as I approached, I failed to see the soft glow of the red and green neon light in the window and—more ominous still—I smelled nothing. Hunan K, it turns out, had been shuttered by the marshals at some point since my last visit. A cryptic sign alluded to some sort of unsatisfied debt and offered the name of the landlord. After more than a decade of Chinese-food stability in my life, I was without bearings. Worse, I'm sure I'll never learn the fate of my friends.

Farewell, Hunan K.

CHAPTER 3

Southeast Asian

Indochine: Vietnamese from war to Wilmington

Solange Thompson was born and raised in Hue, Vietnam. Her mother, who had left school by the third grade, was fiercely dedicated to Solange's education, sending her to Saigon to St. Paul's convent, where she learned French and English. Solange not only finished high school; she graduated from Mhanvan College in Vietnam. Soon after, in late 1960s, she relocated to Thailand to escape the instability of the Vietnam War. While living in Bangkok, she pursued a career in public relations, working part-time in her godfather's restaurant and the rest of the time in an antiques shop. She also met U.S. Air Force Captain Bob Thompson.

They married, had their first child (they would later have two more), and at the end of the war relocated to North Carolina's Cape Fear Coast—the cluster of towns and beaches near the city of Wilmington—to live near the local military base, where Captain Thompson was stationed. This was in 1973, and the only Asian restaurant in town was a Chinese restaurant that was as bad as one might expect a Chinese restaurant to be in Wilmington, North Carolina, in 1973.

Solange had never heard of North Carolina. When her husband explained the move, she asked, "Is it in New York?" Nothing could have prepared her for the size of the United States or for the remoteness of the North Carolina coast, which today is a day's drive from Washington, D.C., but was even more isolated before the completion of Interstate 40 in the 1990s.

One day, while Solange was working at the antiques shop in Bangkok and fretting over her impending departure, an American woman made a purchase and asked to have it shipped to a North Carolina address. Solange asked if that address was anywhere near the base where they were headed. It turned out that she and the woman were to become neighbors and, over the years, close friends. But things weren't so pleasant at first.

Solange remembers arriving in North Carolina to rainy, gray weather. She asked where the local market was, assuming every town in the world had a bustling outdoor market with fresh produce and seafood vendors, and was directed to the A&P, where everything came in cans. The only Asian ingredients she could find were rice and La Choy soy sauce. She sank into a depression.

Over the course of that first difficult year, Solange found comfort in cooking. A Southeast Asian community had established itself in Washington, D.C., so occasional trips there provided the taste of home and some ingredients she could carry back to Wilmington. She started teaching cooking classes a couple of times a week in her kitchen, and she acclimated to life in the United States, making new friends and over time becoming something of a local celebrity. Throughout the 1970s, '80s, and '90s, Solange operated a few restaurants, mostly Chinese with a few Southeast Asian dishes on the menu—whatever the local market would tolerate. She also worked in the antiques business and amassed quite a collection of Asian artifacts dating back to the fifteenth century.

There's a unique building on Market Street, just outside of downtown Wilmington. Built in the 1950s for the owner of a cement company, it is an architectural gem, with a copper roof and unusual arched windows enclosing the dining room. It survived every kind of weather and ownership—approximately ten restaurants occupied it over the years—but by 2000 it had fallen into disrepair and was housing an awful American buffet restaurant. Solange had been watching the building for years, because the arches reminded her of Southeast Asian architecture. When the buffet went out of business, she put in a bid and bought the building.

Over the course of a couple of months, Solange remade the building into a Southeast Asian restaurant: Indochine. She filled it with the antiquities she had collected over nearly three decades; she commissioned local artists to paint murals; and her husband, by now retired, did all the landscaping. Once you walk through the front door of Indochine, you're in an environment so convincingly Southeast Asian that you can't believe you're in America. Indochine has exactly the rambling, eclectic ambience of a restaurant at a Thai or Indonesian beach resort. Every table is hand-painted; every wall covered with art and artifacts. In the restaurant's courtyard, a bar, its copper roof resembling layered leaves, shares space with a fish pond and arched wooden structures housing semi-private tables. Inside, a private party room features a real Vietnamese hawker's stand repurposed as a bar.

The menu is Vietnamese and Thai, with guest appearances from other places in Asia where Solange has spent time. Indochine is good not just by North Carolina standards but by any standards. For example, it's a happy coincidence that catfish is an ingredient common to the southern United States. But Indochine's braised Vietnamese catfish, with a spicy-sweet ginger glaze, is the best catfish preparation I've had anywhere, and that can't just be chalked up to lucky geography.

Wilmington has embraced Indochine with tremendous enthusiasm—and it's probably no accident that one of Solange's friends, another Vietnamese woman, opened Wilmington's first Asian market a few years ago. Altogether, the restaurant's various indoor and outdoor seating areas can accommodate about 200 people, and on a busy weekend night Indochine may serve 500 or more customers. The parking lot is jam-packed not just on Friday and Saturday nights but also every weekday for lunch. Local businesses hold meetings in Indochine's private bungalow, and several couples have been married on the wooden bridge over the courtyard garden.

SOMETHING FISHY

Fish sauce and fish paste are universal seasonings—the Southeast Asian equivalents of soy sauce in China or salt and pepper in Western cooking. In Vietnam fish sauce is called *nuoc mam*. In Thailand it's called *nam pla*. In Burma (Myanmar), *ngan byar yay*. In Cambodia, *teuk trei*. In the Philippines, *bagoong*. Fish pastes are popular as well: Indonesian *trasi*, Cambodian *prahok*, Malaysian *belacan*, and Filipino *patis*.

Most Westerners are blissfully unaware that one of the most prevalent and delicious flavors in Southeast Asian cuisine is produced through one of the more disgusting processes in the culinary world. Fish sauce is an extract made from fermented fish. It's typically made from smaller fish and by-catch that have little other commercial value. Some fish sauces are made from a single variety (for example, anchovies), and others are made from an assortment. The method is simple but labor- and time-intensive. As soon as the boats unload the catch, the fish are placed in barrels with a highly concentrated saltwater solution. The barrels are filled with salt, the ingredients are weighted down, and then the barrels are sealed and left to sit for a year or more (in some modern industrial processes, there are ways to accelerate the fermentation), during which time the enzymes in the fish's digestive tract and skin cause fermentation and extraction of the liquids from the fish into the solution. Occasionally the barrels are opened to the sun for a little while to aid fermentation, and the fish are then pressed and reweighted. At the end of fermentation, the liquid is drained or siphoned off from the barrel. Second-rate fish sauce is made by topping off the remains with additional saltwater. The process of producing fish paste isn't all that different, except it's quicker because the fish solids remain in the final product.

Fish sauce isn't something you'd want to make at home. In ancient Rome, a fish sauce called *garum* was a popular seasoning, and home production was actually outlawed because of the foul aroma. When fish sauce is finally siphoned off from the barrels and bottled, however, it has a mellow, salty, complex, subtle taste like none other. Not only does fish sauce impart its own taste to food, but it's also a flavor enhancer. Fish sauce is rich in glutamate, the flavor enhancer, also found in MSG, that imparts the umami taste to foods.

What's Wrong with This Picture?: Why you've probably never been to a Filipino restaurant

According to the 2000 United States Census, five of the top six Asian populations in the United States are:

1. Chinese: 2,734,841 (this number goes up a bit if you also add Taiwanese)
3. Indian: 1,899,599

4. Korean: 1,228,427
5. Vietnamese: 1,223,736
6. Japanese: 1,148,932

There are no other groups outside the top six that come anywhere close. Going down to number 7 on the list, the numbers fall off by a factor of five, to 206,052 for Cambodian—and it's downhill from there.

Looking around at Asian restaurants in America, this list seems logical because population figures should do much to determine the popularity of Asian cuisines. Many people assume that restaurant popularity and ethnic population rankings are in lockstep.

In some cases, that's true. For example, Chinese cuisine is so well established that according to a recent National Restaurant Association study, it's viewed similarly to the other two most popular ethnic cuisines: Italian and Mexican. According to the *Chinese Restaurant News* trade journal, there are 43,139 Chinese restaurants in the United States right now, or 3.37 Chinese restaurants for each McDonald's.

Population does much to explain the popularity of specific cuisines because larger numbers of people from a given ethnic group represent more customers, a deeper pool of restaurant owners and workers, and better supply lines. That's no surprise. Perhaps the most interesting situations, though, are the ones where population doesn't explain the popularity of an ethnic cuisine. There are two examples, in particular, that break the mold.

You may have noticed that I left off number 2 in the list of largest Asian-American populations. Before I say what that group is, take a quick guess.

Most people I've given this test to have guessed Thai. After all, Thai restaurants are everywhere, so there must be a whole lot of Thai people in the United States. But that's wrong. The number 2 group on the list is Filipino.

There are 2,364,815 Filipino-Americans in this country, according to the census. If population truly determines the popularity of restaurants in a strict ratio, there would be more Filipino restaurants than Indian restaurants, more Filipino restaurants than Japanese restaurants, and almost as many Filipino restaurants as Chinese restaurants. Yet there are only 481 Filipino restaurants in the United States, or 1.1 percent as many Filipino restaurants as Chinese.

What's going on here? One simple explanation would be if Filipino cuisine were somehow undesirable—if, for example, it consisted only of dishes based on anchovies. But Filipino cuisine is diverse and delicious, and because of the interactions between the Philippines and Spain, the United States, and its Southeast Asian neighbors, the cuisine is ready-made for American palates.

Perhaps the most prominent Filipino chef in the country is Cristeta Comerford, the White House executive chef. Though she prepares traditional Western cuisine at the White House, she is also an informal ambassador for Filipino cuisine. The *Philippine News*, a newspaper targeted at that community, published an account in 2007 of a Filipino exhibition dinner that Comerford cooked in Washington, D.C. Although nobody has a complete answer to the question of why there aren't more Filipino restaurants in North America, Comerford suggested several factors: first, that Filipinos aren't a restaurant-going culture ("Even in the Philippines," she said, "there aren't many Filipino restaurants"); second, that Filipinos have a strong cultural preference for eating at home with family; and third, that cooking has not traditionally been considered a legitimate career in Filipino culture.

I think there are other issues as well. One is marketing. Many people don't like to think of ethnic cuisines as being the result of marketing—it flies in the face of popular notions of authenticity. But the reality is that Japanese cuisine would not be where it is today were it not for concerted marketing efforts at many levels, from both formal and informal corporate and government sources. Nobody but the president of the company knows just how much money Kikkoman, the global soy sauce manufacturer based in Japan, has spent promoting Japanese cuisine each year for the past several decades, but the sum has surely been staggering.

There is no similar marketing effort under way for the cuisine of the Philippines, and Comerford is not going to accomplish it alone. In addition, for national cuisines to enter the mainstream, there need to be a few dishes for tastes to coalesce around. There doesn't yet seem to be a Filipino equivalent of pad Thai, though there are some legitimate candidates—delicious dishes like *adobo* (pork or chicken in a soy sauce, vinegar, garlic, and peppercorn broth) that should be more popular but just aren't.

Speaking of pad Thai, Thai cuisine is an example of the opposite of the Filipino phenomenon. It is the major outlier on the list of Asian-American populations. There isn't, and has never been, a particularly significant Thai population in the United States; in 2000, the number was just 150,293. Even adding the Laotian (198,203) and Hmong (186,310) populations (many people from those ethnic groups have also opened Thai restaurants) doesn't make a terribly significant total. Yet Thai cuisine is quite popular in the United States, with about 4,000 restaurants here, according to Thai government estimates (about one Thai restaurant for every thirty McDonald's). Surprisingly, they aren't just in the large coastal cities. I recently had one of my all-time best Thai meals at a restaurant called Spoon Thai in Chicago, where dozens of Thai restaurants are clustered in the northeastern part of the city; another memorable Thai meal was one I had in Dallas, at Thai-riffic; and perhaps the most acclaimed Thai restaurant in North America, Lotus of Siam, is tucked away in a strip mall in Las Vegas.

What, then, explains the popularity of Thai cuisine in spite of the population numbers?

American involvement in Vietnam is a factor, because so many Americans became exposed to Thai and Laotian culture during that time. More than a few soldiers returned home with Thai spouses. Moreover, Thai cuisine is quite popular worldwide—it is one of the most successful Asian cuisines in places ranging from Europe to Australia, so there is already a global awareness of and infrastructure for Thai cuisine.

Finally, I think Thai has been the right cuisine at the right time. It's perceived as healthier, lighter, more vibrant than the standard Cantonese-influenced Chinese-American cuisine that's dominant in the West, yet similar enough to be accessible to anybody who likes Chinese food. It's no surprise that Thai items have found their way onto a lot of Chinese-restaurant menus in America, just as sushi has.

Certainly if one had to make a mathematical prediction, it would be that someday Filipino cuisine has to reach critical mass in North America. It feels like a long shot, but the census numbers don't lie. If someone cracks the code to creating Filipino restaurants with mass appeal, it could happen.

CORNERING THE MARKET

The first time I tried boiled peanuts was at the home of my friend Dean, who lives in Raleigh, North Carolina. When he handed the bowl to me, it was more of a dare than an offer. Boiled peanuts, a beloved tradition in the Southeast, are—to put it generously—an acquired taste. To me, they're like salty peanuts that fell into a glass of tepid water and were forgotten for a few days. Surely, I thought, this is just some peculiar fetish of the Old South. And yet boiled peanuts were also invented independently in Vietnam—and therein lies a tale.

When it opened in 1965, the Tryon Mall in Charlotte, North Carolina, was the place to be. Anchored by a Woolco and a Peebles department store, and located in the middle of a thriving middle-class neighborhood, the mall flourished throughout the 1970s. But in the 1980s, as a result of urban blight and outward migration of the middle class, the Tryon Mall atrophied. Woolco gave way to a Winn-Dixie, which gave way to a furniture liquidator, which in turn went out of business. The once-proud Tryon Mall, with its two red pagodalike entrances, was nearly abandoned. As the local paper, the *Charlotte Observer*, described it, "Retailers flocked out. Soon only Family Dollar was left. Weeds sprouted in parking lot cracks. Graffiti decorated walls of vacant buildings. Breezes sent litter scudding everywhere."

A structure in such disrepair, with its pothole-filled parking lot and reputation as a hangout for drug dealers and gangs, would normally be torn down to make way for new development. But in 1997, three Vietnamese-American sisters, Mimi, Ivy, and Megan Nguyen, bought the 130,000-square-foot central plaza of the old Tryon Mall. The Nguyens, owners of a small Vietnamese supermarket called Viet My that had outgrown its original location, had a vision: they would open a large Asian supermarket and rent the rest of the space to other shops and restaurants. After almost two years of unanticipated costs, renovation delays, and disasters—including a flood caused by Hurricane Danny—the new International Supermarket opened and the Tryon Mall was reincarnated as the Asian Corner Mall.

Aside from its now-packed parking lot and the people, mostly Asian-Americans, streaming in and out of the entrances, the Asian Corner Mall still looks a bit like an abandoned mall. Little has been done to repair the parking lot or to spruce up the interior (because Asian Corner occupies only the central section of the mall, there has not yet been an agreement among all the owners about how to share repair costs). But where there were abandoned stores, now there are Asian restaurants, markets, and shops. Current occupants range from the Dragon Court Restaurant and Hong Kong BBQ to the Nguyens' International Supermarket and the newer, larger New Century Market, owned by another Vietnamese-American family, which opened in 2004.

Vietnamese-American customers are an important segment of the client base at Asian Corner Mall, and on Tet (the Vietnamese lunar new year) the mall is packed inside and out with people watching dragon dances and fireworks displays, listening to speeches, and buying goods being sold by churches and charities. One popular offering is little bags of *dau phong:* boiled peanuts.

It was meant to be, I think: Vietnamese-Americans selling boiled peanuts at a mall in North Carolina. And the Vietnamese ones are just as much of an acquired taste as Dean's.

The World of Southeast Asian Restaurants

Every chapter of *Asian Dining Rules* could be its own book, but perhaps nowhere is this more true than with Southeast Asian cuisine. One chapter to cover Thai, Vietnamese, and Cambodian food strains the limits of information-compression, and as a result several other worthy cuisines, such as Malaysian, Indonesian, and Filipino, of necessity fell by the wayside.

Luckily, however, many of the same tactics will serve you in good stead at all kinds of Southeast Asian restaurants, whether those cuisines are specifically discussed here or not. Before proceeding to a description of some representative dishes at Thai, Vietnamese, and Cambodian restaurants, then, here are ten tips for getting the most out of Southeast Asian restaurants in general.

Look for the Offbeat

Most Southeast Asian restaurants in North America in a given genre (such as Thai) will have a core repertoire of dishes that don't vary much from restaurant to restaurant. But many will also have dishes on the menu that fall outside the circle of the familiar. It may be that they're family favorites of the owners, or special dishes of the region from which the chef hails, or dishes that utilize local ingredients (such as crawfish in Louisiana and Texas). It's a good bet that these dishes—the ones that aren't genre standards—are going to be interesting.

Communicate About Spice,
and Communicate Again

Southeast Asian cooks and servers are conditioned to believe that Westerners are lightweights when it comes to hot, spicy foods. When a server asks you how spicy you want a dish, it's not enough to say "spicy." You need to be very specific, and then you need to repeat yourself. If you dare.

Even if you fail completely at getting the kitchen to make your food as spicy as you like it, there's still a fallback plan: condiments. Most Southeast Asian restaurants will place various condiments—including hot chili sauce—on the table. If not, you can ask for them. Real Southeast Asians use condiments all the time to adjust the seasoning of their foods—there's no shame in it. Condiments are also useful if some people at your table don't like spice but others do: all dishes can be ordered mild, and those who want spice can add it. It's not a perfect solution—food cooked with spice as an integral part of the process isn't the same as food with spicy condiments spooned on top at the table—but it does the trick.

THAI SPICY

I thought I had cracked the code. "Thai spicy!" I declared to the waitress at Sripraphai, which is not only the best Thai restaurant in New York City but also one of the very few acceptable ones (for this reason, I suggest you avoid Sripraphai unless you're willing to become jaded about all the Thai places you currently enjoy). She nodded—clearly, this clever turn of phrase (simply saying "very spicy" won't even get you to square one) indicated an in-the-know Caucasian customer who could tolerate spicy food the way Thai people eat it.

It was spicy enough to cause perspiration and some discomfort, but as with all the best spicy Southeast Asian cuisine, the heat was not simply for its own sake but was balanced by the other flavors in the dish. Most great Southeast Asian cuisine—to paint with a very broad brush—is characterized by a balance of tastes, particularly between sweetness and spiciness. It also tends toward the extremely aromatic. In its Americanized incarnations, however, this cuisine can be either sickly sweet or one-dimensionally spicy—the kind of food you eat only on a dare.

Sripraphai is one of the few restaurants in New York that strikes the right balance, and where the dishes give off the aromas of the genuine article. I ordered this same dish, "jungle curry" with one or another meat (most of the dishes on the menu are protein-interchangeable: chicken, beef, pork, tofu), on my next four visits, each time feeling exceptionally proud of myself for having reached across the great cultural divide that so often makes it impossible for non-Asians to get authentic cuisine in Asian restaurants.

And then, on visit number six, I started in on my jungle curry (with chicken this time), and as I was blithely approaching the second bite, I realized that a dull pain was beginning to radiate outward from the roof of my mouth, up my sinuses, and all over my head, which was beginning to throb. I dropped my fork on or near the plate, instinctively drank a glass of water—which only made it worse—and then ate my rice and my wife's rice and attempted to recover.

Eventually the waitress noticed my distress. She apologized, "Oh, sorry, this time I forget to tell chef you're not a Thai person. That one, it's real Thai medium-spicy."

Share Everything, and Say So

The default style of restaurant service in Southeast Asia, indeed throughout much of Asia (though not Japan), is family-style: all dishes are placed in the center of the table and shared. Many Southeast Asian restaurants, however, have adapted to Western preferences and will go around the table taking each person's order, then place each person's food in front of that person. This is just not a great idea: who wants to eat an entire order of pad Thai? One of the great advantages of Asian restaurants is that the larger your group, the more things you get to taste. So be sure to enlist your tablemates—sell the idea hard if you have to—in the enterprise of sharing. And let the server know you'll be sharing everything and would like enough small plates, bowls, and serving utensils to make that possible.

View the Meal as a Whole

The best way to order a Southeast Asian meal is to put together a whole meal purposefully, rather than being guided by the random intersection of everybody's first choice. If there are six people at the table and everybody loves noodles, everybody's first choice is going to be a noodle dish. But who wants an entire meal consisting of six noodle dishes? Instead, take charge of the ordering, assemble everybody's preferences, then negotiate and strike a balance of appetizer/snack items, soup, starch, vegetables, meat, and seafood. Have one person place the whole order. This lets the restaurant's staff know you're serious.

Control the Pace of the Meal

Perhaps the number one customer complaint I hear about Southeast Asian restaurants is that the service is too fast. In part this is due to a cultural divide: in the West we're accustomed, especially in restaurant dining, to eating in courses; in most of Asia, with the exception of formal banquet meals, all dishes are served at once in a veritable avalanche. The less Westernized the restaurant, the faster this happens. This is one instance where I lean against the indigenous cultural behavior: I prefer to have the food served in waves. For one thing, this allows me to always be eating still-hot food. For another thing, usually the table can't comfortably accommodate as many dishes as my group is likely to order. And for still another thing, I like to warm up with a few little snacks, then move on to soup, then have the rest of my dishes. It's not the right way to do it, but I prefer it that way and so do most Westerners I know. The way to make this happen is, simply, to give your order in phases. When you sit down, order a few small items as appetizers (don't necessarily limit yourself to the part of the menu that claims to be appetizers—it's fine to mix and match). Then order some soup. Then, when your soup is delivered, order the rest of your meal.

Favor Specialists

For the most part, a restaurant that specializes in one cuisine is likely to do a better job with that one than a restaurant that serves multiple cuisines. There are exceptions to this rule: the restaurant Indochine, described at the beginning of this chapter, does a great job with both Thai and Vietnamese, and a Chinese restaurant I visited in Canton, Ohio, called Ricky Ly's, has several excellent Thai dishes on the menu. But there are usually explanations for these exceptions: the owner of Indochine grew up in Vietnam and then lived in Thailand before coming to the United States; Ricky Ly has Thai relatives. I firmly believe a conscientious cook can cook anything well, but as a rule of thumb I avoid restaurants that serve multiple cuisines because in most cases they do it not out of love of the cuisine but as a lowest-common-denominator business decision meant to attract the widest possible audience by emphasizing quantity of choices over quality of cooking. In some cases, you may even luck into a niche specialist, for example a Vietnamese restaurant that focuses only on *banh mi* (sandwiches) or *pho* (soup). Such places are almost invariably good at what they do.

Look for Family Ownership

One of the best clues to a conscientious Southeast Asian kitchen is family ownership. I've had my best Southeast Asian meals at small, personal, family-owned and family-run restaurants. The larger, corporate-owned restaurants, which tend to be investments, are not likely to be as subtle in their cooking.

Get to Know the Staff

I've found immigrants from Thailand, Vietnam, and elsewhere in Southeast Asia to be incredibly approachable and outgoing. You'll probably find it easy to make a personal connection with the servers and managers at Southeast Asian restaurants. And you should do that: learn their names, find out exactly where they're from, get them to tell you their stories. You'll be part of the restaurant's extended family in no time.

FAMILY SECRET

This is the story of how I got the name Mr. Spicy Noodle.

There are very few reasons why you'd want to go to court in New York City, but one such reason is that Chinatown begins behind the courthouses.

When I worked as an attorney, and also when I've been on jury duty, lunch in Chinatown has always been the consolation for having to go to court.

Though Manhattan's Chinatown is of course home to many Chinese restaurants, many other types of Asian restaurants also call it home. There are, for example, several Vietnamese restaurants clustered on Bayard Street. Probably the most popular restaurant with courthouse workers is Pongsri Thai, a huge operation that must serve several hundred lunch customers a day.

And then there was Thai Mint. My brother-in-law Jon, then a special narcotics prosecutor, discovered Thai Mint a few days after it opened and concluded that it was superior to the larger, more popular Pongsri Thai. Indeed, Thai Mint never became popular at all, which is probably why it no longer exists. But during its short life, my wife, my brother-in-law, and I dined together at Thai Mint as often as several times a week.

Like many Asian restaurants, Thai Mint was family-owned, but this family was not exactly typical. For example, our regular waitress, Tik, kept her hair military length and always dressed androgynously with suspenders over a man's shirt, long before this style was popular with fashion models. During her downtime, she would sit at a table in the corner reading books about Judaism. One time it came up in conversation that we live near the 92nd Street Y (similar in concept to a YMCA but with a Jewish orientation), and Tik commented, "Oh yes, they have lots of good Jewish books there." When we asked her if she was Jewish, she scoffed. "Me? Jewish? Ha!"

At first we tried various items from the menu, but over time I settled in with number 5, "Spicy Noodle," with a choice of beef, chicken, pork, or tofu. It became my usual, such that I didn't even have to order—Tik just knew that's what I would have.

The menu at Thai Mint had, in the left margin, a ranking system for the spiciness of dishes. One star was a little spicy, two stars medium spicy, three stars very spicy. I would always ask for my spicy noodles spicier than three stars, so Tik called that "Four star spicy!"

One day Tik e-mailed my wife to say she was going to the library at the 92nd Street Y to read some Jewish books, and did we want to come by and say hi. We walked over and met her; then we showed her the Jewish Museum, three blocks west. It was there, one summer day on one of the wrought-iron benches outside the Jewish Museum, that Tik leaned in and whispered conspiratorially, "You know, the chef calls you Mr. Spicy Noodle. Ha!"

Not long after that bonding moment, we headed to Thai Mint for lunch, only to find it closed. "Lost our lease" read the hastily scribbled sign in the window. One cryptic e-mail reply came in from Tik to my wife, concluding with "Say hello to Mr. Spicy Noodle!" And that was the last we heard of Tik or anyone related to the Thai Mint enterprise.

Until now, only six people—my wife and the five-person staff of Thai Mint—have known me as Mr. Spicy Noodle. You can call me Mr. Spicy Noodle too.

Make a Seafood Decision

Though Southeast Asia is surrounded by water and therefore has a rich seafood tradition, many Southeast Asian restaurants in North America just don't get great fish. This can be because of where they're located (it can be difficult to get good-quality, inexpensive, fresh fish in some of the landlocked states) and also because of customer preferences (if few customers order fish, there won't be enough turnover to keep the inventory fresh, so most seafood products will be frozen). So one of the major decisions you need to make at any such restaurant is whether you're going to focus on fish. On your test visit to a restaurant, then, it can be a useful plan to start by ordering a seafood dish right up front, treating it as an appetizer, before you order anything else. If it's made with low-quality frozen shrimp that are tough and flavorless, or with generic supermarket-quality fish fillets, you know you should stick to meat, noodles, and vegetables. If the fish is fresh and delicious, you should order as many fish dishes as possible because, when done right, the seafood dishes of Southeast Asia—enhanced by such flavors as lemongrass, cilantro, and lime—are among the world's finest.

Seek Advice

To find out what's best at a Southeast Asian restaurant, it's smart to ask. But you have to ask a certain way. Servers are programmed to answer the question "What's good?" by reciting a list of the most popular dishes at the restaurant. But what's popular isn't always what's best; otherwise Britney Spears would be one of the greatest singers of all time. So you need to get the server off script and to demand some real opinions. The more specific you can be in your questioning, the more real the answers will be. Instead of asking what's good, ask, "What are some of your favorite dishes?" And state your preferences: "We love seafood, we love spicy, we don't like sweet."

BECAUSE THIS CHAPTER COVERS multiple cuisines specifically, and Southeast Asian cuisine in general, and there isn't space to provide detailed lists of dishes for every kind of restaurant, I've organized the beginner, intermediate, and advanced sections as brief overviews of my favorite Thai, Vietnamese, and Cambodian restaurant dishes, respectively. You'll also find substantial overlap among the cuisines of Southeast Asia—it's an area of many tightly packed nations with interlocking cultures and ethnicities—and, even more so, among restaurant menus. It's possible, for example, to sit with a Cambodian restaurant menu and a Vietnamese restaurant menu and pair up quite a few of the dishes. And some dishes are for all intents and purposes pan-Southeast-Asian, such as *satay* (grilled skewered meats), which originated in Indonesia but are popular all over and appear on Thai, Vietnamese, Malaysian, and several other types of Southeast Asian menus.

I categorize Thai as beginner because Thai food is the most common and approachable of the Southeast Asian cuisines represented in North America. Vietnamese is somewhat less popular (unless you live in certain places, like Texas) but still pretty widely available, so I classify it as the intermediate cuisine. Cambodian cuisine, because it's harder to find and doesn't have a standardized English-language menu, is what I've called advanced. For each I've listed just a few basic dishes to get you started: these are the items I'd recommend you order if you have no familiarity with the cuisine. Once you establish a comfort level, it's time to start exploring the rest of the menu.

BEGINNER: THAI

To the extent that there can be a defining characteristic to something as diverse as an entire nation's cuisine, Thai cuisine is typified by a balance among hot, sour, salty, and sweet flavors. Most of the cuisines of Southeast Asia make some use of those four poles (perhaps the best Southeast Asian cookbook in English, by Jeffrey Alford and Naomi Duguid, is titled *Hot Sour Salty Sweet*), but Thai cooks have elevated the balancing act to an art form. Not every dish contains all four flavor components, but as long as you order a variety of dishes, the overall meal should still reflect the essential balance.

In addition to fish sauce (nam pla), ingredients that make up the flavor profile of Thai cuisine include lemongrass, Thai basil (more floral than typical Western basil), kaffir lime leaves, coconut milk, garlic, ginger, and galangal (a relative of ginger whose pungent flavors shine especially well in soups).

Thailand, formerly known as Siam, has never been conquered, and its culinary culture has traditionally shown less Western influence than most other Southeast Asian cuisines. Thai cuisine does, however, reflect many Chinese and Indian flavors, particularly in Chinese-derived noodle dishes and Indian-derived curries.

The following are my five favorite widely available Thai dishes.

Pad Thai. Although pad Thai is by far the most popular Thai dish in North America, and although it is delicious when made well, it is not exactly typical of Thai cuisine. Pad Thai was introduced to Thailand during World War II and promoted by prime minister Luang Phibunsongkhram as part of a nationalist campaign. So while it has in many ways become the national dish of Thailand, it is a relative newcomer. Pad Thai consists of stir-fried rice noodles with egg, bean sprouts, and usually shrimp, chicken, or tofu or all three. It's seasoned with fish sauce and tamarind and garnished with crushed peanuts and lime. Pad Thai should be light and clean tasting. If the restaurant you order it at serves a sweet, gloppy, ketchupy noodle dish, you're getting an inferior specimen. Noodle dishes, by the way, because of their Chinese origins, are the only dishes commonly eaten with chopsticks in Thailand.

Pad see yew. This is my personal favorite Thai noodle dish. I will always choose it over pad Thai unless I'm in a group large enough to justify two noodle dishes in the order (in which case I might get a double order of pad see yew!). On menus, pad see yew is usually called "soy sauce noodles" in English. It's made from broad rice noodles stir-fried in a mix of dark soy sauce and fish sauce, with Chinese broccoli, garlic, egg, and a choice of sliced meat. It has a great balance of flavors: in particular, the Chinese broccoli provides interesting bitterness to balance the sweetness that the soy sauce brings to the dish.

Larb. Also sometimes written "larp," larb is a Laotian dish that's popular in Thailand. Since most of the Laotians who've opened restaurants in North America have opened Thai restaurants, here this dish is associated with Thailand, not Laos. Larb is essentially a salad with finely chopped meat. It can be made with chicken, beef, pork, or just about any other meat, which is mixed with chilies, mint, ground toasted rice, and vegetables and garnished with lime and fish sauce. It's served at room temperature.

Tom kha gai. This will often appear on menus in English as something along the lines of "chicken soup with ginger, coconut, and galangal," or "lemongrass chicken soup." However it's described, if it's made well, it's one of the world's great soups. Pieces of chicken are served in a broth made of coconut milk infused with ginger, galangal, hot chilies, and lemongrass. Sometimes there are also other herbs, as well as mushrooms, in the soup—not every restaurant makes it exactly the same way.

Curry dishes. Thai curries reflect the Indian influence on Southeast Asian cuisine, but they have their own identity. You're likely to see several curries on a typical Thai restaurant menu: yellow curry, green curry, red curry, Massaman curry, Penang curry, and in some restaurants, sour curry and jungle curry. Each of these is based on a different curry paste recipe. Basic ingredients common to most Thai curries include fresh chilies, lemongrass, galangal, garlic, shallots, kaffir lime, and cilantro. The branches to red, green, yellow, and beyond depend on the proportions of the ingredients and the addition of other herbs and spices. A finished curry dish is built up from the curry base, to which other ingredients, such as coconut milk (though some curries, like sour curry and jungle curry, use water, not milk), are added. The more conscientious restaurants often make their own curry pastes, which are the freshest and most vibrant; most restaurants buy prepared pastes, which can be quite good too. You'll need to do some experimenting to see which you like best. My favorite is Penang curry, which is made with sliced beef in a sauce that has a particularly thick consistency (it's one of the few curries that's served on a plate rather than in a bowl), thanks to palm sugar and coconut milk.

JUDGING A BOOK BY ITS COVER

When the Time Warner Center—a gigantic upscale vertical shopping center occupying several stories of an office building complex—opened on Columbus Circle in Manhattan, it met with a lot of resistance from dyed-in-the-wool New Yorkers who kept saying, "Nobody will want to eat in a mall." A few years later, the ambitious restaurants in this particular mall have prospered beyond anybody's expectations, and the refrain has evolved to "I hate eating in that mall."

Contrast that with Asian restaurant culture, which seems to have no hang-ups about location. For example, the office tower at 211 East 43rd Street is one of New York City's most nondescript, a relic of the functionalist period when great efforts were made to design buildings just ugly enough to be ignored without being remembered. But in the basement of 211 East 43rd Street, where most buildings stockpile their trash and tend to the boilers, lies a Japanese restaurant so full of character that it stands as one of the great proofs of the "Don't judge a book by its cover" maxim.

I learned about Saka Gura a while back, when Tom Colicchio, then the chef of Gramercy Tavern (and a man of few words), whispered in my ear, "Saka Gura is where I eat Japanese." I cleared my calendar, ditched my deadlines, and hailed a cab. After walking up and down 43rd Street between Second and Third—three times—I finally asked the security guard at number 211 if he knew where Saka Gura was. "Basement," he said, bored.

I followed a trio of mini-skirted Japanese twenty-somethings down the fire stairs and through a humble wooden door, and there it was: Saka Gura, a thoroughly Japanese subterranean expat hangout, faithful in every detail right down to the American jazz music and the awful paper lanterns. The bar offers more than 200 varieties of sake, the Japanese brewed rice "wine." Saka Gura is well documented in Japanese-language guidebooks and websites, but it gets only token attention from the American press—usually whenever sake is the topic of the moment.

In Asia, it seems that nobody gives a second thought to restaurants in basements or in vertical malls. Where else are they going to put restaurants in cities like Tokyo and Singapore, where the population density makes Chicago look rural by comparison? In Asia, it seems the attitude is that the restaurant experience does not begin until you enter the restaurant.

This aesthetic has carried over to the New World. Traveling around North America, time and again I've encountered wonderful Asian restaurants in the most unappealing locations. Sun Luck Garden resides in a Cleveland strip mall ("turn left at the KFC"); China 46 inhabits a former Greek diner in a Day's Inn parking lot on Route 46 in Ridgefield, New Jersey. The main architectural feature of Sripraphai, in Woodside, Queens, is white venetian blinds from Home Depot; from the outside, it's hard to tell if the restaurant is even open. Conversely, I've had some memorably awful meals at places where all the money must have gone into the design, rather than into the ingredients or the kitchen staff.

INTERMEDIATE: VIETNAMESE

The Vietnamese are masters of contrast, particularly of texture and temperature. Most of my favorite Vietnamese dishes juxtapose crunchy and silky, hot and cold, or raw and cooked. For example, many dishes are topped with crumbled peanuts after cooking, and raw bean sprouts are frequently used as a garnish for soups. There's also a bright acidity to many Vietnamese dishes, thanks to ingredients like vinegar and lime juice.

Vietnamese cuisine has been heavily influenced by the longtime French presence in Indochina: Vietnamese sandwiches (banh mi) are served on baguettes, and coffee (iced, with sweetened condensed milk) is a popular beverage. Here are my five favorite Vietnamese-restaurant dishes.

Pho. Probably the best-known Vietnamese dish in North America, pho is served in more than 1,000 restaurants in 47 states, according to the "National Pho Restaurant Directory" at www.phofever.com. The word *pho* is also part of the name of many Vietnamese restaurants and is fertile ground for wordplay (as in the restaurant "Mo' Pho'" in New Jersey). Pho is a noodle soup with a distinctive beef-and-herb broth that's relatively clear in appearance (the richness of the broth can come as a surprise, given its light consistency). It can be eaten for breakfast, lunch, dinner, or a late-night snack. Half the fun of eating pho is garnishing the bowl with fresh bean sprouts, chilies and chili sauces, fresh herbs (like cilantro, basil, and mint leaves, which you tear up and throw in the broth), and lime juice (you're often given a wedge you can squeeze yourself). In areas with large numbers of Vietnamese immigrants, there are often restaurants devoted to pho and other soups, but most every Vietnamese restaurant has pho on the menu. The specialty shops, however, are likely to have many more varieties of pho available, such as with beef, chicken, beef meatballs, tripe, or offal.

Banh mi. We don't typically associate Asian cuisine with crusty bread, much less baguettes. But the French influence in Vietnam left behind a love of baguette sandwiches. Like pho, banh mi can be found in small specialty shops (indeed, many pho shops serve banh mi as well) and also at some regular Vietnamese restaurants. The baguette for banh mi is usually made with a blend of wheat and rice flours. It bears aesthetic similarities to the salad-filled sandwiches you'd find in the French countryside, except that the ingredients have an Asian inflection.

There's usually a main meat ingredient topped with thinly sliced pickled carrots, daikon radish, onions, and cilantro. *Banh mi thit nuong* is made with grilled pork, usually seasoned with lemongrass. *Banh mi ga* is with sweet glazed chicken (similar to teriyaki). *Banh mi xiu mai* is with sweet pork meatballs. *Banh mi bi* contains shredded pork skin with toasted rice powder—a crunchy, bacony combination. *Banh mi trung* is made with scrambled eggs cooked like an omelette. And *banh mi chay* is vegetarian, usually with grilled tofu.

Bun. This is the Vietnamese term for rice vermicelli (angel hair) noodles. The Vietnamese have adopted these noodles with vigor, and most Vietnamese restaurants offer multiple permutations, either dry or in soup. The standard dry selections might include room-temperature bun topped with chicken, pork, beef, shrimp, or spring rolls.

Goi cuon and cha gio: summer rolls and spring rolls. There's sometimes confusion on the definitions of summer rolls and spring rolls, because many restaurants, on account of language barriers, mislabel them. It's easy, however, to tell the difference: summer roll (goi cuon) skins are room-temperature and soft; spring roll (cha gio) skins are fried and crispy. Vietnamese spring rolls are not all that different from Chinese spring rolls, except for the garnishes. You'll be given a plate of lettuce leaves: wrap the spring roll in the lettuce, then dip it in various sauces. Spring rolls are delicious, but the summer rolls are where the real action is. Summer rolls start with rice-paper skins, which are filled with a main ingredient (shrimp, chicken, or pork, usually), a handful of soft rice vermicelli, mint, cilantro, basil, lettuce, chopped scallions, and shaved carrots. They're usually served with peanut sauce and lime wedges. They also happen to be one of the great summer picnic foods.

Goi du du. Papayas, before they ripen and turn yellowish orange, are green. Like unripe tomatoes, when papayas are in their green phase they serve as a crunchy vegetable. Goi du du, or green papaya salad, is common to many Southeast Asian cuisines. (There are also salads made with green mango.) The dressing is usually made from fish sauce, lime, and sugar, and toppings can range from beef to shrimp. Garnishes are typically cilantro and crushed peanuts. If you order this—or any other Vietnamese dish with peanuts—as a take-out item, it's best to ask for the peanuts on the side so they don't get soggy.

THE HIDDEN COST OF TAKEOUT

When I was in law school, my friend Jon and I used to study late into the night, and we'd order delivery from a place called Dumpling King. In addition to having very good (as one would hope) dumplings, Dumpling King had the fastest delivery of any restaurant I'd ever experienced. Compared to Dumpling King, Domino's Pizza is the slow boat to China, a zeppelin to Dumpling King's stealth fighter.

Since we had never been to the restaurant in person, we imagined that Dumpling King was actually a mobile restaurant kitchen in a van. We theorized that as soon as the kitchen's supercomputer detected our call, its artificial-intelligence algorithms plotted our location on a map and started driving toward us at a high speed, a team of cooks yelling and clanking on their woks while trying to maintain their balance through the sharp turns, the computer all the while asserting control over traffic signals and monitoring the police radio band. By the time we relayed the order to the woman on the phone, and she tabulated the price and reported it back to us, they were ringing the buzzer to come up to the apartment with steaming hot food. Or at least it felt that way.

Like many residents of cities and the denser suburbs, I've relied on Asian-food delivery for sustenance for much of my life. In my neighborhood, there's even one restaurant that delivers the food of multiple Asian cultures as late as 2 A.M. But I never gave much thought to the human element of the delivery process until one day when I called Saigon Grill, our favorite local Vietnamese delivery place, during a major snowstorm. The lady on the phone said, "Pick up only!" and I figured it was because of the weather. But when I trudged through the snow to pick up the food, I asked some questions and was told, "Deliverymen on strike!" I couldn't get answers to the "why" questions, though.

As I compared notes with several fellow Saigon Grill aficionados, it became clear that the restaurant's delivery workers had gone on strike in response to allegedly inhumane and illegal working conditions. While my first, selfish reaction was alarm at no longer being able to sit around in my underwear and order Number 19 (*goi du du*, green papaya salad with beef), the situation eventually got me thinking.

The circumstances under which restaurant delivery workers labor—particularly Asian-restaurant deliverymen—are brutal. These are not the spoiled-rotten union workers at the hotel restaurants, who shriek when their pedicure benefits are placed at risk. The Asian-restaurant delivery guys risk their lives every time they set out on those bicycles and mopeds. They're paid almost nothing (the concept of the minimum wage hasn't quite filtered down to all the immigrant communities), and their tips can be unpredictable—if they even get to keep them. Historically these workers seem to have been almost completely unorganized and to have fallen outside the notice or protection of any agency or group. A *New York Times* article about the Saigon Grill delivery strike introduces us to twenty-three-year old Jian Xie. He makes thirty to forty deliveries a night, going as many as forty blocks (eighty blocks round-trip, which in New York City is approximately four miles) by bicycle to deliver a single order. One night, according to the article, he was held up at gunpoint and lost $300 of the restaurant's money. He was required to compensate the restaurant for the loss.

As consumers, we are partly to blame for this state of affairs. We demand rock-bottom prices and have incredibly high expectations for speedy delivery. When the weather gets bad, we order more. In cities, where the competitive environment is fierce, if the price of beef lo mein goes up a dollar at one place, we can order from five other places in the same delivery radius—and many of us do just that. We expect free extras like cold noodles and sodas. And because the price of the food is so low, even a generous tip isn't all that much as an absolute number. There's only so much money a deliveryman (in my lifetime I've never seen a woman delivering for an Asian restaurant) can make $2 at a time.

Soon after the Saigon Grill delivery workers went on strike, a nearby Chinese restaurant, Ollie's Noodle Shop and Grille, was sued by its delivery workers. The Ollie's workers claimed the restaurant was violating minimum wage laws, paying them as little as $1.40 an hour. Other restaurants in New York, such as a downtown Asian noodle restaurant named Republic, have been hit with lawsuits as well. The Asian American Legal Defense and Education Fund is getting involved in several lawsuits, bringing unprecedented legal resources to bear on the situation. One reason for this increased activity, it turns out, is that many of the delivery workers are recent immigrants from the same few towns in China's Fujian Province, so they're able to compare stories and coordinate action.

It's not hard to see that this sort of legal action and collective bargaining is going to start happening more and more. As immigrants assimilate, they're increasingly unwilling to accept sweatshop conditions. Asian restaurants that are out of compliance would be wise to get ahead of the game and get their employment practices in order, because once a restaurant gets into a big labor dispute involving back wages and penalties, the costs really mount. Most restaurants can't survive that.

For our parts, we'll have to pay more for the food. That's the price of humane working conditions. Though I may not look forward to a $2 increase in the price of beef lo mein, it's a small expense on behalf of responsible labor practices.

ADVANCED: CAMBODIAN

Cambodia and Vietnam are neighbors, and their food cultures are closely related. Most Cambodian dishes have Vietnamese counterparts, and vice-versa. Cambodian cuisine, however, tends to be more rustic than Vietnamese. Cambodians particularly love sour flavors, and when Cambodian dishes are spicy, they're seriously spicy.

While the cuisine is ready-made for North American audiences, Cambodian restaurants are probably the most difficult to navigate of the Southeast Asian restaurants found here. There aren't all that many of them—though some areas, like Lowell, Massachusetts, have high concentrations—and the menu spellings and naming conventions are far from standardized.

Many dishes on a typical Cambodian restaurant menu have equivalents in Thai, Vietnamese, and other Southeast Asian cuisines. For example, you may see several "kari" dishes on the menu. *Kari* means "curry," and these dishes should be familiar enough to you if you've eaten much Thai food.

Amok. The name of this dish gives rise to many "run amok" jokes; indeed, I can't remember the last time I read a review of a Cambodian restaurant that didn't contain at least one "amok" pun. Amok is a signature of most Cambodian restaurants and consists of fish in thickened coconut milk curry (the seasoning, called *kroeung,* consists of, among other things, hot chilies, garlic, galangal, lemongrass, and fish sauce). The experience of eating amok is similar to eating a Thai curry dish, except because the amok has been steamed, it has a lighter texture. Other versions of amok, such as chicken amok (*amok saich moan*), may also be available. In such cases, the standard amok may be called *amok trey* to indicate that it's the fish version. Some Cambodian restaurants also offer *amok chouk*, which is made with snails.

Katiev. Most people who get into Cambodian food develop a strong position on how to spell "katiev." One alternative is "kuy thiew"; another is "kuyteav." The actual pronunciation goes something like "k'theeyoo," so take your pick. In any case, it means "noodle soup," and Cambodian noodle soups are my favorites of all the Southeast Asian soups. Because there are no standardized recipes, specific ingredients vary by restaurant—even in Cambodia, ten different katiev vendors might use ten different recipes. The most popular is Phnom Penh katiev, which usually has at least five ingredients in the mix. At my favorite Cambodian restaurant, the Phnom Penh katiev contains ground pork, shredded duck, sliced chicken, whole shrimp, and flat rice noodles in a rich chicken broth. But your local Cambodian restaurant may make it with a pork broth and different ingredients, or it may be a beef broth similar to Vietnamese pho.

Num banchev. Often called just "Cambodian crepes" on menus, these rice-flour crepes are available with a variety of meats and ingredients, such as pork, fish, shrimp, or vegetables, and you get to roll them up yourself. The batter for the crepes is a mix of rice flour, coconut milk, water, egg, sugar, salt, turmeric, and chopped scallions. In addition to the crepes and the main ingredient, you'll be served a plate of garnishes that typically includes lettuce, bean sprouts, fresh herbs, crushed peanuts, chili sauce, and a fish-sauce-and-vinegar dressing.

Salor kor-ko sap. This thick vegetarian soup, really a stew, contains a variety of produce including eggplant, bitter melon, pumpkin, green banana, and assorted greens in a base of coconut milk, water, lemongrass, galangal, kaffir lime leaves, turmeric, and garlic. It's often referred to as the national dish of Cambodia, though it's less popular overseas in part because the bitter melon flavor—which appeals to the Cambodian sour tooth—takes some getting used to.

Nhoam. The word *nhoam* just means "salad," but one Cambodian meat salad has achieved particular prominence in restaurants in North America. It's often called *lap Khmer* (Khmer beef salad) on menus and is typically listed under the "nhoam" heading. Ultra-thin slices of raw beef (or, in some cases, beef that has been seared just a bit) are fanned out on a large plate, like Italian carpaccio. Then they're smothered in an avalanche of fragrant ingredients that usually includes thin slices of onion, finely chopped string beans (or long beans), lime juice, garlic, lemongrass, fish sauce, sugar, mint, basil, and chilies. It's a great dish to start a meal with, as it really wakes up the palate.

IF A PICTURE IS WORTH A THOUSAND WORDS, HOW MANY WORDS IS A "FOOD SAMPLE" WORTH?

All across North America, they look the same: a long, narrow space with a counter at the back; behind the counter is the kitchen, and above the counter is a menu board with color photos of many of the dishes. These hole-in-the-wall restaurants can be found in cities and suburbs everywhere, nestled between office buildings, or between the dry-cleaner's and the pet store in a strip mall.

I love that so many Asian restaurants show photos of their food. It's a sensible way to remove much of the ambiguity from the ordering process. Not only do photos short-circuit unnecessary interrogations, they transcend language barriers.

I particularly love the encyclopedic photo book at my favorite Thai restaurant, Sripraphai, in Queens, New York, where they have a photograph of every single dish on the very long menu. I don't even use the words; the photos are my menu. Because the restaurant serves so many dishes that aren't available at the average Thai restaurant, without that book I wouldn't even know which is a soup and what comes on a plate. I wouldn't know which fish come whole and which are served as fillets. I'd have never figured out that dish number O-2, "Chicken with ginger sauce over rice," is the same as the popular Singaporean/Malaysian specialty of Hainanese chicken rice—something I'd

been searching for and craving for years, ever since
visiting Singapore.

But if a picture is worth a thousand words, how
many words is a sculpture worth? The Japanese have
taken the visual representation of food to the highest
level with their glossy replicas known as "food
samples." In the Kappabashi-dori shopping district
of Tokyo, there are entire stores that sell nothing
else. The phenomenon started in Japan in the 1920s,
when the replicas were constructed from paraffin
wax, which made for beautiful samples that were not
particularly durable. Today, vinyl chloride is the
general material of choice; resin is used for the most
intricate designs. When it comes to high-quality
Japanese food samples, every piece is made by hand.

If you search around online, you'll find a wonderful
video called *The Making*. It's just about the most
astonishing thirteen minutes and fifty-eight seconds
you'll ever spend at your computer. The video has
no spoken words, just a synthesized Japanese music
sound track and Japanese subtitles. The camera
takes us inside a food-sample production studio,
where the techniques used in making facsimiles is in
many ways more impressive than actual cooking.
Using flexible molds, a microwave oven, an airbrush,
a blow dryer, and various cutting tools, artisans
make fake food that's often more appetizing than
the real thing. It's fascinating to watch the food
materialize, starting with white liquid vinyl and
developing into a finished product. The craftsman
pours the liquid into a long thin mold—What will it

be? It's the body of a shrimp! Then the tail is made in another mold, painted, and attached to the body. The attention to detail is profound: when making the food sample of shrimp tempura, the craftsman painstakingly paints the coral-colored striations on the shrimp's body, only to cover it in a golden tempura crust so that only the shrimp's tail is visible.

Then there's the Grand Sichuan book. A picture may be worth a thousand words, but the Grand Sichuan book actually is several thousand words. The restaurant, Grand Sichuan International Midtown, closed long ago. I have, fortunately, preserved a copy of the book. The detailed, sometimes inscrutable, descriptions of dishes were clearly a labor of love on the part of the owners. You may think you know all you need to know about prawns with garlic sauce, but think again:

PRAWN WITH GARLIC SAUCE: The fresh prawn marinated and sauteed with garlic sauce, thicken, strong and spicy. In Chinese, garlic sauce actually means "fish smell sauce". The sauce was invented by ancient Sichuanese. Long long time ago, Sichuanese ate a lot of fish. Sometime they didn't finish the fish dish and saved it for the next day. Then they mixed the fish and other dishes and other dishes had the fish taste and delicious. Sometime in Winters they could not catch the fish. Then Sichuanese wondered if they could make some sauce with the fish taste to satisfy their appetizing for fish. As a result, the Sichuanese invented the fish smell sauce: garlic sauce. The good garlic sauce has the fish's taste and smell without any fish ingredient. The real garlic sauce is called fresh garlic or mashed garlic.

It's odd that the traditions of food photos, samples/sculptures, and lengthy descriptions have never taken hold in Western restaurants. Perhaps there's a puritanical impulse at play here—the same bias that refers to beautiful photographs of food as "food porn." There appears to be no equivalent phrase in Asian cultures. Western culture has even rejected lengthy descriptions of dishes. Restaurants are routinely derided in the Western food press for listing the sources of ingredients and details of preparation beyond the simplest phrases.

Photos, models, and encyclopedic descriptions are just some of the things Asian restaurants do that all other restaurants should do too. Any restaurant that serves family-style should copy the Asian-restaurant practice of having a lazy Susan in the middle of the table. And, of course, every restaurant everywhere should give out hot towels.

Tiny Kampuchea: Finding your inner Khmer

Of all the people I interviewed for this book, I felt the most immediate connection with Ratha Chau. We're both thirty-somethings, we like the same restaurants, and we get each other's jokes. We're each the father to one child: a two-year-old son. To be sure, there are differences as well. I spent my early childhood in New York City under the Ed Koch regime; Ratha spent his in Cambodia under Pol Pot. When I was a kid, I said farewell to my father, an English professor, and went off to summer camp in Connecticut. When Ratha was a kid, he said good-bye to his father, a four-star general in the Cambodian army, who was taken off to a prison camp in Vietnam for eighteen years.

Ratha, his two brothers, and their mother escaped Cambodia and eventually wound up in Connecticut, where he lived a typical American teenage life. His English is perfect and unaccented: speaking to him on the phone, you'd never guess he wasn't a white guy from the 'burbs. After graduating from Clark University, Ratha and one of his brothers started a seafood exporting business and spent a few seasons selling Maine sea urchins to buyers in Japan. Eventually Ratha got into the restaurant business—not as a cook, but as a manager. Before starting his own restaurant, he was the managing partner at a well-known French restaurant in Manhattan called Fleur de Sel. But the flavors of home were calling to him.

Kampuchea restaurant (*Kampuchea* is the Khmer word for "Cambodia") sits at the corner of Rivington and Allen streets on Manhattan's Lower East Side. It's the only Cambodian restaurant in New York City right now. There

should be a lot more. Cambodian cuisine is elegant, sometimes lusty and sometimes restrained, but always balanced
and usually healthful. If you want to find Cambodian
food in the rest of the country, though, you really have to
look for it.

Kampuchea is tiny, just 900 square feet on the main
level—that includes both the dining room and the open
kitchen—and a prep area in the cellar. It's my first visit.
When I enter the tiny kitchen, I almost step right into a
man-size opening in the floor. Having narrowly escaped
the fall, I look down to find a metal staircase—almost a
ladder—going down to the prep area. There are no hand-
rails. Though he's six feet tall and broad of shoulder,
Ratha scurries down the ladder-stairs with the agility of a
spider and expects me to follow. I place my foot on the
first step, brace my arms against the side of the hole in the
floor, and start down. Eventually there are things on either side of the staircase to hold on to. By the time I claw
my way down, a small line has formed. Two cooks quickly
scale the stairs carrying massive tubs of ingredients, like
it's no big deal.

One day Ratha lets me take on the task of making the
house chili-lime-tomatillo hot sauce. He provides me with
latex gloves and offers protective eyewear. "Don't rub
your eyes," he cautions. The kitchen is so minuscule that
wherever you stand, your back is against a stove, a stock-
pot, or an oven. The hot sauce starts with whole limes,
peeled but with some of the white part of the rind left on
(this adds a little desirable bitterness to the finished sauce).
The limes are liquefied in a blender (this requires a lot of
pulsing and knocking around of the blender, because
Ratha—a purist in this, as he is in many things—is ada-
mantly opposed to adding any water). Then a fistful of

whole little green bird's-eye hot peppers—small but mighty—is also pureed. Then several whole tomatillos, also blended into the mixture. After a few repetitions we have a bucket of the stuff. Then Ratha pours a cup or so of it back into the blender and adds garlic, ginger, mint, and red onion, and we combine that with the main batch. Then a lot of salt and a little bit of sugar. "A little sugar balances the sauce. It makes all the difference. A lot of chefs don't like to admit they use sugar—there's a stigma attached to it—but most of them do," says Ratha, an eerie echo of my late father-in-law explaining why he always added a little sugar to his chicken soup.

The hot sauce is great when fresh out of the blender, and about an hour later the flavors meld into a more unified sauce. This isn't something Kampuchea uses as a part of any dish—they just give it to you as a condiment on the table if you want hot sauce. Preparation for 5:30 P.M. dinner starts at 9:00 A.M., and much of that time is spent making complex sauces and condiments that most customers don't think about twice.

At 4 P.M. it's time to shop for flowers. There's only one floral arrangement at Kampuchea, at the end of the tiny bar/counter by the kitchen, but Ratha wants it to be beautiful. He prefers a live flowering plant and doesn't trust anyone else to pick it out for him. It's the hottest day of the summer. "Let's walk up to the Union Square greenmarket," Ratha says, and before I can respond he's out the door. Union Square is about a mile from Kampuchea. I trail Ratha like a miniature poodle being dragged by its owner. I keep joking about how this is just like the weather in Cambodia. Ratha laughs the first couple of times. As I wonder whether I'll survive the journey, we pass by a plant store and Ratha spies a potted plant with little pale yellow flowers. He negotiates down from $35 to $30, carries the plant back to Kampuchea, repots it in a square black planter on the bar, and goes off to finish the chicken stock.

Kampuchea specializes in a variety of noodle soups and has a stock-making operation that rivals that of a much larger restaurant. The Kampuchea chicken stock is the most concentrated, extracted chicken stock I've ever had in a restaurant. First, chicken is simmered in water; then that chicken is removed and new chicken is added and simmered to create a double stock. But this double stock is made with a very low ratio of water to chicken parts, so it's super-rich. For the first round, 200 pounds of chicken parts (five 40-pound buckets) go into the filing-cabinet-size pot, with water just barely to cover. The second simmering calls for 120 pounds of chicken along with onions, garlic, ginger, carrots, and celery. That's one stock for one day of this tiny restaurant's operations. They also make a beef stock and a vegetable stock.

Of course, the chicken soup is amazing. If you didn't see the stock being made, you'd be tempted to say the richness and concentration of the broth was achieved through some sort of trickery. It isn't. All you're getting in the chicken soup is that super-rich broth garnished with a little lime-leaf oil—plus the noodles, chicken meat, and whatever else goes in the particular soup you ordered.

Just before the dinner service, Ratha takes his lunch break. There's little privacy at Kampuchea, so he usually goes up the street to a Dominican restaurant called El Castillo de Jagua and has a tuna sandwich.

It's 5:30 P.M. and the first customers of the evening arrive: a couple with a baby in a Bugaboo stroller. They place their order, which a waitress keys in to the Micros touch-screen computer. A split second later, a little printer in the kitchen spits out an order ticket: one shrimp crepe, one catfish crepe (crepes are a mainstay of Cambodian cuisine). Ratha is down in the hole in the floor, and his chef-de-cuisine, Scott Burnett, is at the stove cooking in four skillets at once. Scott barks: "What's on the ticket!" I read it off, and Scott reflexively says, "Oui, chef!" before realizing it's only me.

As the activity dies down, Ratha gives me a look. He's evaluating me, sizing me up for something. Finally he nods and asks, "Are you ready to become an honorary Cambodian?" If you're a member of PETA, please stop reading now.

It turns out that Kampuchea has a small, occasional supply of embryonic duck eggs—in other words, duck eggs that are almost but not quite hatched. In one of the most extreme eating experiences of my life, Ratha and I eat one together. It's an alarming, disorienting, wonderful, delicious, disgusting, awe-inspiring, remorseful, celebratory moment. The egg is poached, the top cut off, and a little lime and vinegar dressing is added. I won't go into an exact description of the taste, texture, and appearance—part of the joy and horror of this experience is the surprise of it all—but yes, there are feathers involved. I just keep telling myself this has got to be an easier way to become Cambodian than living through Pol Pot and war with Vietnam.

Every cook in the restaurant has gone through this Cambodian hazing ritual. If you handle the duck egg without passing out, you earn the title "Honorary Cambodian," sort of the Cambodian equivalent of BFFs ("best friends forever"). If you call Ratha and arrange it in advance, and swear to secrecy, he may be willing to prepare one of these eggs for you. Just don't tell anyone.

A SENSE OF HUMOR

When a Westerner orders a meal at a restaurant, the selection of dishes comes down to what's likely to taste good. In traditional Asian cultures, however, a meal is about much more than just flavor. It's about a holistic approach to wellness that dates back to ancient times.

Throughout Asia, different cultures practice variants of the Chinese and Indian philosophies wherein the proper balance of bodily "humors" (such as "fluid," "blood," and "vital energy") is thought to be the key to good health. In particular, many Asian cultures categorize all foods as either "heating" or "cooling"—designations that have nothing to do with temperature and can appear random to outsiders (for example, tea is considered to be cooling). This dovetails with the belief in yin and yang, the notion that the world hangs in the delicate balance of positive and negative energies. A balance of heating and cooling foods is required in order for a meal, or a day of eating, to be physically and spiritually healthful. Herbs can also be used to influence the balance of the bodily humors, and traditional Asian medicine is heavily oriented toward the use of herbs to address various ailments and deficiencies.

It was against this historical background that one day I found myself at the Imperial Herbal Restaurant in Singapore, the only restaurant I've ever been to where a doctor of herbal medicine prescribes your meal. Upon our arrival, my wife and I were led into the office of the herbalist-in-chief. He started with my wife. He took her pulse, examined her tongue, looked her over, and started asking questions. "Do you have trouble breathing? Heartburn?"

He was right on both counts. He took out a sheet of paper and wrote character after character of Chinese calligraphy. It was a prescription for an herbal remedy that she could get filled by any Chinese herbalist. He also told our waitress what herbs to add to my wife's food, and what dishes she should eat.

It was my turn to take the chair. The herbalist looked at my tongue, took my pulse, and said, "Okay. Thank you." And he got up to leave.

"Aren't you going to write me a prescription?" I asked as he walked toward the door.

The herbalist wheeled around and said, "You don't need a prescription. You're too fat. You just need to eat less and exercise more."

He was right about that too.

CHAPTER 4

Korean

Strong Women: Korean food joins the mainstream

Bibimbap, the popular Korean dish of rice garnished with mixed vegetables, egg, chili paste, and sometimes meat, is often served in a dolsot, which is a hot stone bowl. A very hot stone bowl: so hot it browns and crisps the rice in the bowl and can easily cook an egg with its residual heat. I'd occasionally wondered how they get the stone bowl so hot, and so when I learned I was going to get my shot at spending some time in the kitchen at Do Hwa, the Korean restaurant on Carmine Street in Greenwich Village, I knew that was to be my first question.

I never got to ask it. As soon as I entered Do Hwa's kitchen I saw a stone bowl, filled with rice, vegetables, and beef and topped with an egg, sitting on the stove. It was right on the burner, and the burner was turned up full blast. It had never occurred to me that it would be as simple as that. But it raised another question: how do they get the bowl off the stove?

The answer was similarly anticlimactic. I imagined there must exist some sort of specialized stone-bowl-grabber contraption, which perhaps had to be special-ordered from South Korea. But in reality the cook, Mrs. Bae, simply grabbed two dish towels, folded them over a couple of times, and used them to grab the bowl off the stove. She placed the bowl on a wooden tray, and within moments, a waitress whisked it off to a waiting customer in the dining room.

Do Hwa is owned by Jenny Kwak and her mother, My-ung Ja Kwak. Before coming to America in the 1970s, Jenny's mother had owned two small restaurants in South Korea (the restaurants specialized in soup). Jenny's father, trained as an artist in Korea, took his first job in New York at the Port Authority Bus Terminal, cleaning Grey-hound buses. Jenny grew up in a single room with her parents and two younger sisters. Late at night, her father would set up an easel and a small lamp in the corner of the room and paint. The smell of paint still triggers these childhood memories for Jenny.

Before Do Hwa, Jenny and her mother had an earlier venture, called Dok Suni, which they recently sold after an almost-fifteen-year run. Dok Suni, which is Korean for "strong women," was instrumental in bringing Korean cuisine into the New York mainstream. At a time when the restaurants in the Little Korea neighborhood were not user-friendly and catered primarily to Korean customers, Dok Suni opened in the hip, trendy East Village and tried to bring Korean home cooking to a mostly non-Asian clientele. Jenny, who was only nineteen when she and her mother opened Dok Suni (she dropped out of the Parsons

School of Design, where she was studying painting, in order to open the restaurant), is also the author of the book *Dok Suni: Recipes from My Mother's Korean Kitchen*.

I dined at Dok Suni several times throughout the 1990s. I had just graduated from college (Jenny Kwak and I are very close in age), and Dok Suni was the first really accessible Korean restaurant I'd found. It was not, however, the first I'd dined at. The high school I went to in New York City, a specialized math-and-science high school called Stuyvesant, had a very high percentage of Asian, and particularly Korean, students (Jenny Kwak's business partner, Christine Park, it turns out, was one of my schoolmates; another was the actress Lucy Liu, who occasionally dines at Do Hwa). Several of my friends in high school were children of Korean immigrants, and I'd occasionally be taken—either by my friends or by their families—to the Korean restaurants on West 32nd Street, Manhattan's Little Korea, in the shadow of the Empire State Building.

I remember the food exploding with new flavors, I remember what seemed like dozens of little plates of food being placed on the table in rapid-fire succession, and most of all I remember the thrill of cooking meat right on a tabletop grill. But I also remember being totally overwhelmed. The menus were in Korean, the servers spoke Korean, and I (like most mainstream Americans at the time) knew nothing of Korean food. So I let my friends order, and I just went along for the ride. It took me four years of occasionally visiting Korean restaurants to get to the point where I could take a group of non-Koreans to dinner and order up an acceptable meal. (This chapter will show you how to do that on your first visit.)

One of Dok Suni's regular customers was the director Quentin Tarantino; he invested in Do Hwa, which opened in 2000. While Dok Suni was a terrific restaurant for its time, Do Hwa is far more elegant, with better facilities and a more ambitious menu.

All the cooks and servers at Do Hwa are women. There are some male dishwashers and bussers, but it's a female-dominated shop. Perhaps because of the feminine influence, Do Hwa has the calmest restaurant kitchen I've ever been in. Even when orders are pouring in from the dining room, nobody yells, clanks, or panics. And there is a feminine, serene feel to the place overall. Christine Park, one of Jenny's longtime friends, oversees the dining room along with Jenny and is as gracious and collected a hostess as I've seen anywhere.

As at many Korean restaurants, some of the tables at Do Hwa have recessed grills in the center. These grills have become perhaps the most identifiable trait of Korean restaurants in North America. Korean barbecue, as it is called, has been gaining popularity in the past decade, and for good reason: it's approachable (Americans love beef), it's delicious (how can you go wrong with thinly sliced marinated beef strips seared on a grill?), and most of all it's great fun (both cooking it and making the lettuce wraps, called *ssam*, in which it's typically eaten).

Korean cuisine, however, is much more than Korean barbecue. So while this chapter will tell you all about barbecue, we'll also go beyond.

Koreans in America: A hundred years of fortitude

Korean restaurants are relatively new to North America, but Korean people have been here for more than a century.

The first immigrants came to Honolulu in 1903 and several thousand followed, to work as laborers in Hawaii. The Immigration Act of 1924, however, closed the borders to further Korean immigration until the time of the Korean War (1950–1953).

Two pieces of legislation, the War Brides Act and the McCarran-Walter Act, were instrumental in increasing the number of Korean-Americans. Many United States servicemen married Korean brides during the war, and the War Brides Act allowed them to naturalize here. The McCarran-Walter Act allowed some Asian professionals and students to immigrate, and many Koreans took the opportunity.

As with many Asian groups, however, the most significant wave of Korean immigration has occurred since the passage of the Immigration Act of 1965 during the Johnson administration, accelerating in the 1970s with further relaxed regulations. Koreans were the most enthusiastic group to respond to the act; in several of the years soon after the act passed, as many as a third of all Asian immigrants came from South Korea.

Many Koreans in this third wave were highly skilled and educated, but in many cases their lack of English language skills made it impossible to find jobs as lawyers, doctors, professors, and engineers. So many of these former professionals instead started their own businesses. Korean-Americans (and Korean-Canadians, particularly in Toronto's Koreatown) opened grocery stores, dry cleaners, and restaurants.

In cities with significant Korean populations, like Los Angeles (which has the largest Korean population outside of Korea) and New York, the Korean independent-business culture supported Korean restaurants. Many Korean businesses are either open twenty-four hours a day (such as many small groceries) or engage in commerce at night (many dry cleaners truck their clothes out to larger facilities that clean the clothes overnight). Korean restaurants met the needs of Korean business owners by staying open twenty-four hours a day. To this day, it's possible to go to restaurants in the Koreatowns of metropolitan North America at 4 A.M. and find them packed with Korean-Americans either getting off work or just starting their day.

Understanding Korean Restaurants

Korean restaurant menus can be overwhelming to the uninitiated, and in immigrant areas you'll find examples that are untranslated or so poorly translated as to be unhelpful: they're written in Western characters, but they don't mean much. This is made all the more difficult by the lack of any real agreed-upon English spelling for most Korean culinary terms (a system called McCune-Reischauer attempts to standardize spellings, but it is not widely used by restaurants), so it's common to find the g and k, j and ch, d and t, and b and p used to mean the same thing. For example, the dish *kalbi* is just as often written as *galbi,* and *panchan* is often written as *banchan.*

Once you start internalizing the vocabulary on any given menu, however, you can decipher many of the items even if you've never seen them before. The same words repeat in various places and usually mean the same thing. It can be a fun logic game.

Before defining the dishes you'll come across on Korean-restaurant menus, though, here are ten tips for getting the most out of the restaurants.

Move Beyond Barbecue

Korean barbecue is one of my favorite things to eat, but there are two problems with focusing only on barbecue when you go out to eat at a Korean restaurant. First, barbecue is just one tiny part of Korean cuisine. Both Americans and Koreans love it, which is why it has become by far the most popular and readily identified mainstream Korean food, but it's just the beginning. If you want to have the most interesting, fulfilling, balanced Korean-restaurant meals, you'll need to move beyond barbecue. Second, Korean barbecue is expensive. It relies on high-quality beef and therefore has a high food cost, which you as the consumer have to bear. You can run up the tab quickly if you order a few kinds of barbecue. If you eliminate barbecue from the equation, or order a small amount to share as a side dish, you can have tasty, filling Korean meals for much less money.

Ask Lots of Questions

Of all the Asian cuisines covered in this book, Korean seems to have remained the most "foreign" to Westerners. There are some Korean restaurants—especially outside of areas dense with Korean immigrant populations—that have developed mainstream presentations. And one of the most acclaimed young chefs in America right now is David Chang, the restlessly creative Korean-American chef of the hip New York restaurant Momofuku. But most Korean restaurants still focus on serving Korean customers.

The basic background knowledge that most people in North America have with respect to Chinese or Japanese food isn't present in Korean restaurants. And there is no clear standardization of menus or even the names or spellings of dishes. Menu translations can be, at best, iffy. The solution is to ask lots of questions. Expressing interest in Korean cuisine and asking for explanations of the different menu items is a terrific way to broaden your horizons. You may find, however, that your server isn't equipped to explain the menu fully in English, in which case you should seek out a manager, who will likely have better language skills.

Go at a Slow Time

The most common complaint I hear about Korean restaurants is that people feel rushed. An avalanche of food comes all at once, and before you know it, the check arrives. I've personally found Korean restaurants to be the fastest-paced of the major types of Asian restaurants in North America. There are two reasons for this. First, culturally, that's just the way Koreans expect their restaurants to be. Perhaps in part because Korean restaurants in North America got their start feeding rushed, busy Korean workers, the pattern stuck. Second, as a matter of expediency, when Korean restaurants get busy, things move very quickly. A high turnover on busy weekend nights is essential to the bottom line. The best way to manage this phenomenon, then, is to go when the restaurant isn't very busy and to ask for a slower pace (or dole out your order in two or three waves, a practice that will likely be accommodated on a slow night). In addition, when dining on a slow night, you'll have many more opportunities to ask questions and interact with management.

Learn the Vocabulary

You'll have a huge leg up if you can internalize the vocabulary of Korean-restaurant menus. While English translations may vary or be absent, most every Korean-restaurant menu has transliteration: the Korean words sounded out in English. While there are some variations (as in *galbi* and *kalbi*, and *banchan* and *panchan*), once you filter out those minor differences, you can identify the dishes no matter how strange or absent the English descriptions are. You can use this book as a cheat sheet at first, but you may find that cumbersome, so eventually you'll want to use your memory instead.

Do It Yourself

At many Korean restaurants, the default behavior with Western customers is for the service staff to do a lot of the things that Korean customers are expected to do for themselves. For example, if you're served a bowl of bibimbap and you have a non-Asian face, chances are the server will present the bowl and then mix it up for you. That's a good time to say, "Oh, thanks, but we'll do that ourselves." Not only does this give you more control over the exact amount of hot sauce you add, but it also lets the staff know you're not just another clueless table sleepwalking through Korean cuisine. Likewise, when you're served barbecue, it's likely that your server will try to push it all onto the grill, then come back a few minutes later and flip it around, then serve it up to you. That totally defeats the purpose of having a grill on the table. Instead, say you'd like to do it yourself. Of course, if you've never done any of these things before, you'll want a demonstration. In that case, be sure to ask the server lots of questions and ask for explanations and tips so you can do it yourself next time.

Determine the Specialties of the House

While the typical large Korean restaurant in a major city will have an extensive menu covering most of the major facets of Korean-restaurant cuisine, not every restaurant makes every dish well. In-the-know customers, especially Korean ones, zero in on a few dishes that each restaurant does well. The challenge is finding out which dishes those are. You could, of course, just order every dish at every Korean restaurant in town and figure it out for yourself, but you can save some time in various ways. First, do some research. The Internet is rife with blogs, discussion forums, and restaurant reviews. You may find that people have dined at all the restaurants in your town and done the legwork for you. Second, if you know any Korean foodies, ask them which dishes they get at which restaurants. Make sure you write down detailed names and descriptions, lest you're unable to figure out which dish it is on the menu. Third, ask a manager at the restaurant. Don't just ask "What's good here?" Rather, ask a question that indicates you know the score; for example, "Which dishes do your Koreans customers think are better here than at other Korean restaurants?" You may not get a truthful answer 100 percent of the time, but sometimes you will. At one of my favorite Korean restaurants in New York, when I asked a manager that exact question, he raised his eyebrows and adopted our table.

Take Advantage of Lunch Specials

Korean food can get expensive, especially when you're in the learning phase, so there's some risk to experimental ordering. Many Korean restaurants, however, have bargain lunch specials targeted at the business crowd. For around $10, you should be able to get a full meal at lunchtime that includes a main plate plus a number of side dishes, or a bento-box-like assortment of dishes. This is a great way to taste a lot of food without spending much money. Then, when you return for dinner, you'll already be a whiz at ordering.

Eat Korean Food

A lot of Korean restaurants have followed the money and installed sushi bars. Some also have sections of the menu devoted to simplified stir-fry dishes meant to appeal to Western palates. These dishes can certainly be good, but they're not be the best way to allocate your Korean dining budget. When ordering at a Korean restaurant, you'll almost always be better served by sticking to the items that are actually Korean.

Ask for Refills of Sides and Condiments

Most Korean restaurants will refill your panchan (little side dishes) at no charge if you ask. So once you've zeroed in on your favorites, go ahead and get more of the ones you like. Try to focus on the items that are not cost-cutters. It's an unfortunate practice in some Korean restaurants that in order to have a large and seemingly generous panchan selection, some items are made from low-cost, uninteresting ingredients. I've seen broccoli stems recycled as panchan, and I almost never touch potato-based panchan items. Also, when you're served barbecue or another dish that comes with an assortment of condiments, you won't necessarily be given enough of those accompaniments to carry you through the entire dish. You don't have to ration them. When you run out, or just before you run out, ask for more. Ask for more rice as well, if you like. You may be charged an extra dollar or two for the rice, but for my tastes and the way I eat, most Korean restaurants don't give enough rice.

Take Stuff Home

Though it might not be an official practice, many Korean restaurants sell their kimchi and panchan items by the pint or quart. You'll probably have to ask, because there may not be a printed list of what's available (be sure, also, to establish a price). But certainly, if you think a restaurant has particularly delicious kimchi or some other item, don't hesitate to try to buy some for your kitchen at home.

CROSSED UP

When I arrived at Cho Dang Gol, the Korean restaurant on 35th Street in Manhattan where I was to meet my dining companion, she was already seated. Well, I shouldn't say she was seated, because she had chosen one of those tables where you sit on the floor. Who knew Koreans sat on the floor? I thought that was a Japanese thing, but no, Koreans are big-time floor-sitters. And this table was hard-core. There was no well underneath, as they have in some Japanese restaurants, for the meek to stow their legs. This was just a short table on a hardwood floor, and I was expected to sit with nothing but a flimsy pillow the size of a Korean's rear end for padding.

I thought about asking her to switch to a different table, namely one with chairs, but I confess I was a little embarrassed. I struggle with a weight problem. One of my defense mechanisms is that I get very stubborn whenever anybody implies that my weight might disqualify me from accomplishing something. And, frankly, I wanted to make a good impression on her, as she is the editor in chief of one of the top food magazines.

So, I sat on the floor like it was no big deal. I didn't sit cross-legged—that just wasn't even an option—but I sat the way I imagine they sit in a Bedouin tent or something, you know, with my legs folded under me off to one side. A side-kneel of sorts.

We ordered *Doo boo doo roo chi gi* and *Doo boo dong gu rnag dking* (literally, "Spicy pan-fried kimchi, vegetables, clear noodles, rice cake and handmade tofu on hot stone plate, with or without pork" and "Eight pieces of small pancake mixed with tofu, ground pork, and vegetables, covered with egg") and several other unfamiliar dishes. I allowed her to place the order, and the food was quite wonderful.

Trouble was, just as the first panchan (an array of salady appetizer snacks) hit the table, my left leg started to fall asleep. As the numbness in my leg progressed toward pain, I attempted to keep the conversation going while eating those slippery salads with metal chopsticks. I also had a lot of trouble figuring out how to use my napkin effectively, since I was without a lap.

Eventually, I could no longer stand the discomfort, so I decided to reverse my position. There were a few problems with this plan, though: first, I couldn't get the leverage to do it because I had no mobility left in my left leg; second, I wanted to accomplish this maneuver without alerting her to my discomfort; and third, for whatever reason I have no trouble mustering up the flexibility to side-kneel with my legs to the left, but somehow the side-kneel to the right doesn't work for me—my hips just won't agree to it. Eventually, though, I realized that she couldn't see under the table, so I sort of stuck my legs out straight. It then became a race between restoring circulation in my leg and losing it in the base of my spine. But I had reached an equilibrium of sorts, shifting back and forth between the two positions every ten minutes or so for the duration of the two-hour meal.

After she paid the bill—and I was glad she paid because Korean food can get expensive if you let a food-magazine editor order—I went to stand up. This proved impossible. Unfortunately, I didn't discover the problem until I was halfway up, so I crashed to the ground unceremoniously, plunking down near, but thankfully not on, a table of old Koreans sitting on the floor like it was no big deal, and needed the assistance of a small army in order to assume a standing position.

I walked the editor in chief back to her office, and as we were heading up the avenue she commented, "Boy, my legs are killing me from sitting on that floor for two hours."

BEGINNER: DIPPING A TOE INTO
THE SEA OF KOREAN CUISINE

The six ingredients that most identify Korean cuisine are *dwen jang* (a paste made from salted, fermented soybeans, similar to Japanese miso), *goit chu jang* (a red pepper paste), sesame oil, sesame seeds, soy sauce, and garlic. Many dishes contain all of these flavors, and certainly most whole meals contain several repetitions of each. Once you develop a taste for the aromatic mixture of dwen jang, goit chu jang, and sesame, you may find yourself craving Korean food at odd hours. Good thing so many Korean restaurants are open late.

The typical Korean restaurant in North America will offer a selection of appetizers, an array of barbecue items, and a few popular nonbarbecue dishes, especially rice dishes.

Korean Barbecue

By far the most popular and well-known Korean food in North America is Korean barbecue. The "barbecue" designation is a bit of a misnomer, since the food is usually cooked on a flat metal griddle (charcoal grills are rare in restaurants, due to fire codes and the effort required to maintain them). However, the name has stuck.

Korean barbecue is a cook-it-yourself meal. First you choose what meats (or other items) you want to cook; then you're brought an array of panchan (little appetizer/snack/side dishes) and platters of the raw items you're going to cook. You place the raw food on the griddle and occasionally flip it and move it around until it's cooked to your liking. Most of the items come sliced pretty thin, and the griddles tend to be quite hot, so the cooking is usually a matter of just a couple of minutes. Your server may help you out if you seem not to be familiar with the procedure. Once the meat is cooked, you wrap it in fresh lettuce leaves with various condiments such as thinly sliced garlic, rice, and a spicy sauce called *ssamjang*.

There are several types of Korean barbecue. These are the ones you're most likely to encounter.

Bulgogi. The term means "fire meat" and refers to thinly sliced beef that has been marinated in a mix of soy sauce, sesame oil, garlic, and other seasonings. By default bulgogi means beef, though you can also get pork (*dweji bulgogi*), lamb (*yang bulgogi*), or chicken (*dak bulgogi*) at some restaurants.

Kalbi. Thinly sliced marinated beef rib meat. Kalbi and bulgogi are the two most popular Korean barbecue items, and for good reason: they're delicious. Kalbi is a particular favorite of mine because of its supremely beefy taste and almost gelatinous texture. Some restaurants offer variants of kalbi such as *wang kalbi* (*wang* means "king," and the pieces of meat are larger) and *seng kalbi* (without the marinade).

Sam gyub sal. Sometimes described as "triple layer pork," this is uncured bacon, sliced thick. Many Americans think it's too fatty, and it does look very fatty, but if you close your eyes and concentrate on the sweet, melting tenderness of the pork you'll understand that the fat is a good thing.

OTHER BARBECUE ITEMS, USUALLY marinated in soy sauce, sesame oil, and garlic, include *jaeyuk gui* (thinly sliced marinated lean pork), *se chi gui* (beef tenderloin), *saewoo gui* (marinated shrimp), *dak gui* (sliced marinated chicken breast), and *ohjingau gui* (sliced marinated squid).

BARBECUE MISTAKES TO AVOID

Korean barbecue actually involves grilling, as opposed to the long, slow cooking typical of American southern barbecue. It is prepared on a tabletop grill and is fundamentally simple: you put the meat on the grill, flip it over after a minute or two, then serve it after another minute or two. It's the most elemental kind of cooking over a flame, but you need to be organized and to behave like a real chef. Here are the five most common newbie mistakes and how to avoid them.

Insufficient Preheating of the Grill

In almost every Korean restaurant I've ever been to, the tabletop grill has not been satisfactorily preheated by the time the raw meats have been brought to the table. So wait. You want that grill screaming hot before you put anything on it. A good way to test it is to take a few drops of water from your water glass and flick them on the grill. If they vaporize almost immediately, the grill is ready. You can also place a mushroom or a slice of onion on the grill before you cook anything else. Seeing how it cooks will give you the information you need to manage the grill going forward.

Cooking Before Everybody Is Ready

Korean restaurant meals too often feel hurried. But when eating Korean barbecue, there's no need to give in to the pace set by the restaurant. After all, you're the chef. You get to decide when to start cooking, and how much to cook at a time. So just because the grill is hot and there's raw meat on the table doesn't mean you have to start cooking. Be sure to learn where the grill's controls are (if it's a gas grill—for charcoal you'll just have to wait it out) so you can turn it down for a while if you're planning to wait before you start cooking. If you've ordered appetizers, wait until your group has finished them and the plates have been cleared before you start the barbecue phase of the meal. And if a server keeps coming by, trying to help you get the meat started on the grill, politely refuse the offer of assistance.

When you are finally ready to start grilling, one insider trick is to season the grill with an onion slice before cooking. Take a slice of onion with your tongs and put it on the grill, then use a circular motion to "wipe" the whole grill several times with the onion.

Cooking Too Much at Once

Much of the reason Korean barbecue is so delicious is on account of the browning of the meat that occurs on the grill. The meat, however, has usually been sitting in a marinade, so it tends to be pretty wet. Thus, in order for the desirable browning to happen (called the Maillard reaction in kitchen-science terms), there needs to be plenty of opportunity for the excess liquid to run off, and the meat needs to make plenty of contact with the grill. So cook your barbecue in very small batches. That way you can spread the meat all over the grill for maximum surface contact and, therefore, the best browning. If you've also heeded the advice to get the grill good and hot before cooking, you'll find that this combination—a superhot grill cooking very small batches of meat spread over the grill's surface—allows you to get excellent browning while not overcooking and drying out the meat. If you play your cards right, you can get a nicely browned exterior and a medium-rare center—the way to go. In addition, cooking just a little bit at a time allows you to give a small portion to each person. Then everybody can eat a little, and when they're ready, you can cook another round.

Putting Too Much Stuff in Your Wraps

You don't eat Korean barbecue straight, like a steak. You'd not only be doing it wrong, you'd also quickly run out of meat. Rather, once the meat has been grilled, the correct procedure is to incorporate it into a wrap. These wraps are called *ssam*. You'll be served a basket of lettuce leaves and possibly herbs like perilla leaves (at least at the better restaurants), as well as white rice and a tray of condiments that may include hot chili sauce, miso paste, raw garlic, and slices of hot chili pepper. Take a lettuce leaf and some herbs, and create a wrap with rice, meat, and the other condiments. But don't jam-pack the wrap full of rice and meat. A well-crafted ssam is a delicate, minimalist object, with just a little bit of filling.

Trying to Ration Your Condiments

You may be served only five or six lettuce leaves with your barbecue. Don't worry. Nobody is expecting you to divide your barbecue into five equal parts in order to create overstuffed ssam. Nor are you required to ration your condiments to make them last throughout the barbecue. Instead, use as little meat and as many condiments as you like in each wrap; then ask for more lettuce and condiments. It's not unusual for my groups to go through three rounds of lettuce and two rounds of condiments before we're done with our barbecue.

Rice Dishes

Bibimbap literally translates to "mixed rice," and in its standard restaurant form, it comes as a bowl of rice with vegetables, beef, and an egg. Sometimes the rice is served separately, and you mix the rice, along with chili paste, into the bowl. Korean restaurants often offer several varieties of bibimbap, such as *sanchae bibimbap*, which comes without meat.

Many restaurants also offer *dolsot bibimbap* (also sometimes called *gopdol bibimbap,* which means the same thing): the *dolsot* or *gopdol* is a stone bowl, heated to sizzling, in which the rice and toppings are served. The best part is the crusty rice stuck to the bowl: be sure not to leave it behind, as it acquires a delicious flavor from the sesame-oil-coated bowl (many Koreans mix some tea in with the last of the rice to make a kind of soup). Variants include vegetarian, seafood, mushroom, and kimchi-and-mushroom.

Other Popular Items

Mandoo are Korean dumplings. Most restaurants will only offer *mandoo* and *kimchi mandoo*. Both contain pork, beef, or a mixture of pork and beef, plus diced tofu and vegetables. Kimchi mandoo also contain spicy cabbage. Some restaurants offer a larger selection, including vegetable mandoo and seafood mandoo. Mandoo are usually served pan-fried but also sometimes can be had steamed or in soup.

Pajun are pancakes similar to the scallion pancakes served in many Chinese restaurants, but larger and filled with more than just scallions. Mixed seafood is the most popular version, and kimchi-filled pajun is also often on menus.

Panchan

One of the things I enjoy most about dining at Korean restaurants is the selection of *panchan*. At the typical Korean restaurant in North America, you'll automatically be served several of these small side dishes at the beginning of the meal. Their interesting flavors and textures build anticipation for the meal and can be enjoyed throughout, and they're free!

The first time you see an array of panchan, it's likely to be an overwhelming experience—like trying to read a foreign alphabet. Over time, as you learn the names and flavors of the dishes, you'll gradually become fluent in panchan. If you don't know what something is, ask your server for both the Korean word and a description of the ingredients (then go home and look it up online for confirmation and suggested spelling). Eventually, when the little dishes of panchan hit the table, you'll be able to rattle them off like a pro.

You can very often judge a restaurant by the quality of its panchan. Chances are, if they take care with the panchan, they'll take care with everything else. If you finish a given panchan item, you can always ask for a refill. Most such requests are happily accommodated, and panchan are intended to be enjoyed throughout the meal. Some items are very salty and best saved for later, when you can have them with some plain white rice. If you don't know what it's called, be sure to leave a tiny piece in the bowl so you can show your server: "More of this, please!"

The following are some of the panchan items you're most likely to see on the table, though there are hundreds of other possibilities. All these selections are likely to be served at room temperature—even the fried ones.

Kimchi (sometimes written "kimchee"). If there is a national dish of Korea, kimchi is it. If you just say "kimchi," you'll be understood to mean spicy, fermented cabbage. However, there are a variety of other kimchi preparations, usually indicated by hyphenated descriptions. For example, *manul kimchi* is scallion kimchi, *oh-e kimchi* is made with cucumbers, and *kaktugi kimchi* is made with radish cubes. There are many other kinds of kimchi, some of which are barely recognizable as such, but cabbage, scallion, cucumber, and radish are the ones you're most likely to see in a restaurant's panchan assortment.

SAY "KIMCHI!"

When Koreans pose for photographs, they don't say "Cheese!" They say "Kimchi!" In many Korean households, there's a separate, specialized refrigerator used only to store kimchi. There's even a museum in Seoul that's devoted entirely to kimchi. It's called the Kimchi Field Museum, and its curators have documented 187 varieties of kimchi: 25 kinds made from cabbage, 62 from radish, 10 from cucumber, and 21 from assorted other vegetables.

The most commonly seen variety of kimchi begins with napa cabbage that has first been salted and allowed to sit for several hours. The cabbage is then rinsed, dried, and spread with seasonings, usually Korean red chili powder, scallions, garlic, ginger, and a little fish sauce. It's then sealed in crocks or plastic tubs and left in a cool place to ferment for several days or weeks.

The basic process of preparing kimchi is not complex. Then again, neither is baking bread. It's the details and tricks that make the difference between mediocre and great kimchi, and it takes practice to get it just right. Expert kimchi makers will sometimes move the kimchi to less cool areas, or let it sit with the lid off for a time, in order to modulate the flavor profile.

Kimchi is often eaten straight, as an accompaniment to a meal. But it is also an ingredient in many Korean dishes. In particular, leftover kimchi that has been in the refrigerator for a while and is losing its desirable texture and flavor is often used in fried rice *(kimchi bokkeumbap)* or soup *(kimchi chigae)*.

In 2006, the magazine *Health* named kimchi one of the world's five most healthful foods. Not only does kimchi have high levels of vitamins A, B, and C, but it is also chock-full of lactobacillus, the bacteria also found in yogurt. Various medical studies have shown a variety of benefits from lactobacillus: it aids in digestion, it helps prevent yeast infections, and it may even reduce the risk of certain types of cancer.

Odeng. A type of fish cake, usually served in long, thin slices. I can't say I'm a huge fan of odeng, and I've found that most Americans (including a lot of Korean-Americans) aren't either. Still, it's worth a taste. The consistency and flavor remind me a little of gefilte fish, a Jewish specialty that I also don't love.

K'ong namul. Bean sprouts seasoned with sesame oil, salt, garlic, chopped scallions, and sesame seeds.

Shigeumchi. Spinach seasoned with sesame oil, soy sauce, and garlic.

Doo-boo chorim. Fried tofu seasoned with soy sauce, sugar, and garlic.

Yeunkeun jorim. Seasoned lotus root. Lotus root is easy to recognize: it's served as thin, round slices with almost a wagon-wheel pattern of holes in each slice.

Hobak jeon. Fried zucchini.

Gamja jorim. Tiny potatoes simmered in sweetened soy sauce.

Gamja saladu. Korea's (not very convincing) answer to potato salad, sometimes made with long, thin shreds of potato, mayonnaise, and assorted garnishes.

NOT YOUR AVERAGE KOREANS

There are three Korean-American–owned grocery stores within one block of my Manhattan apartment. There's the OK Market, which is open 24/7/365, which I can use to amaze my out-of-town friends with instant procurement of chips, dip, and ibuprofen at 4 A.M. There's the Patrick Murphy Market, which has that name because the current Korean-American owners bought it from a guy named Patrick Murphy, who was not Korean. And there's the Apple Tree Grocery, which doesn't specialize in apples or even have a very good selection of them but has the nicest owners of the three.

In the past three decades, Korean-American–owned grocery and convenience stores have spread throughout much of the United States. In California, for example, Korean-Americans now own more than 48 percent of grocery and convenience stores. The National Korean American Grocers Association (called KAGRO) counts 25,000 stores as members. In cities where Korean greengrocers are common, such as New York, where there seem to be four at every intersection, many people now refer to their local small markets as just "the Koreans," as in "I'm running down to the Koreans to get some milk."

But there are Koreans and then there are Koreans. The Super H-Mart in Ridgefield, New Jersey, is to my local Korean markets as the *Queen Mary 2* is to a rowboat.

Walking into the Super H-Mart is like slipping into a parallel universe where everything is just a little bit off. It looks just like the larger suburban supermarkets found all over North America, but the products are unfamiliar; many of them aren't even labeled in English. Whereas the Korean greengrocers in many cities are oriented toward providing basic Western products to mainstream customers, the Super H-Mart serves a primarily Asian clientele and specializes in Korean and other Asian products. There are now sixteen H-Marts (some Super, some not) in six states.

Where a Western supermarket might have a produce rack devoted to a few kinds of lettuce, Super H-Mart has a several-hundred-square-foot area devoted to more kinds of greens than I can differentiate with the naked eye. A mainstream supermarket might have a few kinds of rice in small bags on a low shelf, while Super H-Mart has stacks of sacks of rice, as large as fifty pounds apiece, both domestic and imported from just about every country in Asia I've ever heard of. It would take at least a couple of hours just to read the labels on every type of soy sauce on offer, assuming you could read several Asian languages.

We recently took our two-year-old son, PJ, to Super H-Mart. (It used to be called Han Ah Reum, but they changed to Super H-Mart last year, probably because they got sick of people pronouncing Han Ah Reum wrong.) He quickly became entranced by the puffed-rice-cake machine. This unusual piece of equipment, which looks like a relic from the former Soviet Union, creates puffed-rice cakes in the blink of an eye. After the rice is piped onto a half-dollar-size superheated metal plate, a piston brings down another metal plate with incredible force, making a sound like a misfiring car engine, and out of the machine flies a thin, puffy, six-inch-diameter rice cake. A bored attendant packs the rice cakes in bags of twelve. Any damaged rice cakes get handed out as free samples. PJ ate three.

Farther along, a crew of Korean women was standing behind the counter making kimchi, the women's hands protected by industrial black elbow-length gloves. Gossiping in Korean and laughing all the while, these women seemed to represent an unbroken lineage of kimchi makers stretching halfway around the world.

Super H-Mart also sells kitchen equipment and appliances, everything from rice cookers to kimchi refrigerators. These waist-high, top-loading refrigerators have multiple internal bins that seal shut in order to keep the powerfully scented pickled vegetables segregated, and they're set to temperatures higher than a regular refrigerator so as to accelerate the pickling process. My wife wouldn't let me buy one.

It was time for dinner. Super H-Mart has—in addition to a bakery, a sushi counter, and a mysterious, smoky sports bar hidden behind the liquor section—a Korean food court. There are several restaurant counters circling the food court, but you order everything from a central cashier. It's nearly impossible to figure out what to order, because the information is scattered all over the various menu boards around the court, and there's little in the way of English-speaking help.

After I placed our mostly random order ("Yeah, let me try F-24, is that good?"), I was given three tickets with numbers on them. Then, as the different restaurants finished preparing our food, they flashed my ticket numbers on digital signs above their counters and started yelling the numbers impatiently. I scurried around picking up the food and brought it to a table in the court, where my wife and son were waiting.

Exhausted and disoriented, I collapsed in a chair, and we ate: a big bowl of rice noodles topped with julienned vegetables and hot pepper sauce, a platter of rice topped with assorted mushrooms, and a sushi roll described on the menu board as a "regular roll," which turned out to be anything but regular. It contained pickled vegetables, ham, and egg.

As I staggered back to the car, still overwhelmed by the experience, PJ summarized: "That was nice restaurant."

INTERMEDIATE: FROM HOT POTS TO RAW BEEF

Larger Korean restaurants, especially in areas where there are significant Korean populations, often have staggering menus filled with unfamiliar items. The main categories are stews/soups, noodles, and often an array of assorted special dishes.

Hot Pots

Different restaurants may refer to the same dish as a soup, stew, casserole, or hot pot. However, they're all of a piece.

Sul nong tang: beef stock with thin rice noodles and beef

Kalbi tang: beef rib soup with daikon radish and clear mung-bean noodles

Sachul tang: lamb cubes in a lamb stock

Myung ran tofu jigae: fish roe (from pollack) and tofu in a spicy broth

Hwangtae guk: seafood broth flavored with dried whiting

Daegu maewoon tang: cod in a spicy broth

Haemul sun tofu: mixed seafood and tofu soup

Dwen jang jigae: classic stew/soup of soybean paste and shellfish, such as clams

Mandoo guk: dumplings served in beef stock

Wooguji galbitang: beef short ribs in a spicy broth with radish

Ddaro gukbab: spicy beef soup with vegetables

Noodles

Neng myun: cold buckwheat noodles served in a cool broth, topped with beef brisket and pickled vegetables

Bibim neng myun: similar to neng myun but without the broth, and with a spicy sauce

Jap chae: sweet-potato noodles, usually served with vegetables and sesame oil

Chun chon mak guk soo: spicy noodles topped with pork and vegetables

Sohn kal guk soo: noodles with squash and potatoes in a clam broth

Momil guk soo: thick buckwheat noodles served cold, with soybean-paste soup on the side

Assorted Other Dishes

Yukhwe. A very popular dish among Koreans, this is their answer to steak tartare. The beef is julienned and served raw with an egg yolk and usually shredded Asian pear.

Jook. Many Korean restaurants also offer rice porridge, what in Chinese restaurants would be called *congee*. In Korean it's called jook, and it is usually served in a ceramic crock. *Junbok jook* is rice porridge with minced abalone, and *yachae jook* is with mixed vegetables. Other combinations may also be available.

Nakji bokeum. Stir-fried octopus and vegetables served with Japanese-style udon noodles.

ADVANCED: THE OTHER PARTS

Offal Dishes

Many Koreans love offal, the parts of the animal left over after it is butchered for steaks, chops, roasts, and other standard cuts. These dishes can be challenging, as their flavors are quite strong and they don't necessarily appeal to Western palates or sensibilities. But for the adventurous, they provide great rewards in terms of flavor and interest. Here are a few offal dishes you might see on Korean-restaurant menus, especially in areas with significant immigrant populations.

Seng gan. Sliced raw liver with sesame sauce. Raw liver is very rich in vitamins and minerals, especially iron. In Korea it is believed that this dish improves stamina and vision.

Gan gui. Similar to seng gan (*gan* is liver), but the thinly sliced liver is served as Korean barbecue and you cook it at the table.

Other offal dishes include *yang gui* (sometimes called "beef mountain chain," this is part of the small intestine), *dechang gui* (the large intestine), *youmtong gui* (beef hearts), and *heo mit sal* (thinly sliced beef tongue), prepared in seemingly infinite variety.

Tofu and Vegetarian Cuisine

There are a few vegetarian Korean restaurants in America, and they're worth seeking out because they are vegetarian restaurants a carnivore can love. The vegetarian Buddhist cuisine of Korea is based on roots, grains, and greens, and the dishes are surprisingly flavorful and diverse. Usually served as a multicourse tasting menu, a Korean vegetarian meal is an experience everyone should have.

Koreans are also masters of tofu, serving perhaps the best tofu dishes of any Asian culture. The highlight, when you can find it, is the silken tofu some restaurants make on the premises. It has a custardy texture and is served warm. Silken tofu is written on the menu as *dooboo* or *dubu*. If you've always wondered why tofu, which too often tastes like a kitchen sponge, is such a mainstay of the Asian diet, here's your silky, buttery answer.

WHAT YOU DON'T KNOW ABOUT CHOPSTICKS CAN'T HURT YOU

"Man who catch fly with chopstick accomplish anything."
—Mr. Miyagi, in *The Karate Kid*

Chopsticks are used throughout most of eastern Asia, to varying degrees and for various purposes: as fingers, forks, and shovels—even as pliers. They are ubiquitous in Japan, of course, and nearly so in Korea (with a significant exception; read on) and Vietnam. Chopsticks are less common in Thailand, where their introduction at the table almost always coincides with the appearance of Chinese dishes—appropriately, since chopsticks are a Chinese invention.

The Kuaizi Museum in Shanghai has over 1,000 pair of chopsticks, dating back to the Tang Dynasty, circa A.D. 618 (though chopsticks are much older, dating back 3,000 to 5,000 years). My personal chopstick collection is a bit smaller: I think I have three pair. I imagine, however, that the Kuaizi Museum does not have a pair, as I do, from Empire Szechuan Columbus circa A.D. 1987. These are two long, smooth wooden chopsticks in a red paper wrapper that declares: "Welcome to Chinese Restaurant. Please try your Nice Chinese Food With Chopsticks the traditional and typical of Chinese glonous history and cultual." The back of the wrapper bears the following instructions:

Learn how to use your chopsticks
Tuk under thumb and held firmly
Add second chcostick hold it as you hold a pencil
Hold tirst chopstick in originai position move the
    second one up and down
Now you can pick up anything!
Bamboo Chopsticks
Product of China

Over the next couple of decades, the English got better. As the children of the Chinese-restaurant owners in my neighborhood went to MIT and Princeton, and the word processor with spell-check became ubiquitous, one mistake after another was corrected until it wasn't even a source of amusement anymore. Then, one day, the chopsticks disappeared, and almost every restaurant switched over to those awful ones that come as one piece and splinter everywhere as you break them apart. I miss the old chopsticks, malapropisms and all.

The word *chopsticks* derives from Chinese pidgin English, where *chop chop* meant "fast fast." In actual Chinese, the word is *kuai*; in Japanese, *hashi*; in Korean, *jeotgarak*; in Vietnamese, *dua*; and in Thai, *takiap*. Chinese chopsticks tend to be long and square at the end you hold and round at the business end. Japanese chopsticks tend to be shorter, and they taper to a pointed end (the better to debone fish with). Korean chopsticks are usually made of stainless steel and are typically flat with the width tapering toward the ends. (Many Westerners think Korean chopsticks are the hardest to use, but if you ask Koreans, they can't imagine using any other kind.) In Southeast Asia the chopsticks are long and wooden (or plastic), tapering to a blunt point.

We tend not to think much about chopsticks, but in Asia they're big business. In Japan the average person goes through 200 pair of disposable chopsticks each year. There are 127 million people in Japan. That's—are you ready?—25 billion pair of chopsticks a year. In China they use fewer pair of chopsticks per year, but there are a lot more people. China goes through 45 billion pair of disposable chopsticks a year. Nondisposable chopsticks have their adherents too. At the Japanese department store Takashimaya, I once impulsively bought $50 chopsticks. That's nothing, though. On the everythingchopsticks.com website you can get octagonal red and black layered lacquered chopsticks for $79.99, and on eBay right now the bidding is up to $225 for a set of Chinese ivory chopsticks decorated with carvings of flying cranes. (That's for a set of twelve, though, so it's a good deal.)

Westerners tend to do a few things wrong with chopsticks. And I don't mean they fail to obey the complex etiquette codes of Japan, which no Japanese person actually expects an American to follow. I mean silly things.

For example, I've met many people who insist on using chopsticks in Thai restaurants, in order to be respectful of that culture. However, in Thailand they eat with forks and spoons. The only time you'd receive chopsticks in a restaurant in Thailand would be if it was a Chinese restaurant, or you were being served a Chinese noodle dish. Otherwise, they haven't been using chopsticks in Thailand since King Rama V introduced Western-style utensils back in the nineteenth century. Whenever I've asked Thai restaurant owners in North America why they put chopsticks on the tables if chopsticks aren't used in Thailand, they've told me it's because customers ask for them.

Nor are chopsticks required in Japan to eat sushi. Sushi is often eaten with the hands, and the best sushi chefs I know prefer hands because they do less violence to the sushi than chopsticks. I know when I go to Japanese restaurants and eat my sushi with my hands, the people eating their sushi with chopsticks look at me like I'm a cretin. But the sushi chefs know it's the right way. Eating sushi with your hands also has the benefit of being much easier than eating it with chopsticks.

And all too often, I see people struggling to eat rice off their plates with chopsticks. But you won't see Chinese people trying to do that. China is not a nation of masochists. The way most Chinese people eat rice is from a bowl held up at mouth level. The chopsticks are used to push the rice from the bowl into the mouth. Show up at any Chinese restaurant when the waitstaff is eating dinner and you'll see how it's really done. In Korean dining, however, eating rice with chopsticks from the bowl is poor form; the spoon is the preferred utensil.

By the way, those instructions I quoted, though cute, also happen to be definitive. There's not much more you need to know in order to use chopsticks to pick up something. And if you use them three times a day every day for a few years, you may very well be able to pick up anything.

CHAPTER 5

Indian

Modern-Day Restaurant Moghuls: An Indian empire in Edison, New Jersey

For my twenty-third birthday, my parents gave me a cashmere sweater. One of my friends got a car. Shaun Mehtani got three restaurants. Nice ones: altogether, they cost $4 million to build. But let's start from the beginning.

Sneh Mehtani, Shaun's mother, came to New York from New Delhi in 1971. She was twenty-three years old, Shaun's age as this birthday. Her first job was as a beautician (technically an "aesthetician" or skin-care specialist) with the famed Christine Valmy. Through the 1970s, she worked at a number of jobs with Indian organizations, networking, traveling, and becoming self-educated, before finally winding up as an executive at Air India.

In the late 1970s, some of her contacts approached her with a project: opening an Indian restaurant in the New York Penta hotel. Though neither a chef nor a restaurateur,

Sneh Mehtani was a well-traveled gourmet with a head for business. She took on the project with her husband, Satish Mehtani, who had been working as a civil engineer. He would oversee the real-estate side of the business.

The Moghul Room opened to critical acclaim. It was a trailblazer for Indian fine dining in America, all the more unusual because of its female owner-operator. But at the beginning of the 1990s, when most restaurateurs would have been looking to open additional restaurants in New York or other major cities, Sneh Mehtani looked into her crystal ball and saw the future—in the town of Edison, New Jersey.

Driving along Oak Tree Road, the main drag of Edison and the neighboring town of Iselin, one would be forgiven for wondering what country they were in. From the Patel Brothers Grocery to the Indian Bridal Boutique, there are more than 300 Indian-owned businesses along the route. Since the 1980s, the Indian population of New Jersey has doubled, climbing to well over 100,000, with more than half that number clustered around Edison.

Though the Mehtanis don't own the Oak Tree Shopping Center, they are its most prominent tenants, with four restaurants, a catering hall that can handle events for up to 800 people, and their corporate headquarters. Identifiable from the outside only by a sculpted bronze door, Mehtani headquarters could easily pass for the offices of a bond trader or an international espionage ring, with several employees furiously working phones and computers, placing orders, resolving problems, and planning catered events—especially weddings.

Sneh Mehtani, in addition to running the Mehtani Restaurant Group, plans as many as 300 weddings a year, from New Jersey to California, Puerto Rico, and Bermuda. She started her wedding consultancy, called Your Wedding, in response to the unmet demand of Indian families for elaborate and difficult-to-plan traditional weddings—events that often include multiple ceremonies and meals, and even grooms on horseback. She assembled a SWAT team of chefs and managers able to go anywhere on a moment's notice and work with local hotels, event halls, and suppliers. Wherever they travel, they ship in their own spice blends from headquarters and order the fresh products locally. The company has a total of thirty tandoor ovens, including portable versions that the SWAT teams take to hotels across the country. Due to the intense heat of the ovens, the teams usually set them up and cook the tandoori breads outdoors on the loading docks of hotels and catering halls.

On a single day this past summer, Sneh Mehtani was overseeing three wedding-related events in New Jersey: a 300-person rehearsal dinner at the Mehtani catering hall in Edison, an interfaith (Indian bride, Caucasian-American groom) wedding for 250 at the Villa at Mountain Lakes near Morristown, and a 400-person Muslim wedding reception at the Glenpointe Marriott in Teaneck. As her driver ferries her around New Jersey, she coordinates everything by cell phone. "This is a slow day," she says. "Some weekends we have twenty events."

Even without the wedding business, though, the Mehtani group is a formidable enterprise, and Sneh Mehtani is one of the world's foremost female restaurateurs. The restaurant group has annual gross revenues of $8 to $9 million and employs more than a hundred people year-round (not including an additional sixty to seventy, mostly part-time, for the wedding business, which peaks in the summer). The Mehtanis defy just about every stereotype

Americans hold about Indian restaurateurs, with a female chief executive, ambitious beverage programs, OpenTable online reservations, and websites offering video tours of their venues. Except for their spices and specialty items, they use mostly Western restaurant suppliers. And they charge for quality: dinner entrees run in the high teens, yet on weekend nights the restaurants are so full you can't even get a space in the shopping center's capacious parking lot. The Edison restaurants serve about 2,000 pieces of hand-formed, tandoor-baked naan bread every weekend.

The Mehtanis' first restaurant in Edison was a copy of Moghul in New York. As the restaurant became too popular to meet the demand of its loyal customers, the Mehtani Restaurant Group began to expand. They opened Moksha, a restaurant based on the cuisines of southern India; Ming, a Bombay-style Chinese restaurant; Mithaas, a modern Indian dessert, tea, and snack shop; Mirage, a banquet hall; and just up the road from the Oak Tree Shopping Center, Moghul Express, a pan-Asian fast-food shop that behind its tiny storefront houses the Mehtanis' vast catering kitchen.

Moksha, on the upper level of the shopping center, is one of the few restaurants featuring the regional foods of southern India. Robustly seasoned dishes from the states of Andhra Pradesh, Tamil Nadu, Karnataka, and Kerala are prepared with an emphasis on physical and spiritual well-being. The curvaceous dining room is done up in rich natural woods; bare tabletops, natural wood chairs, bamboo blinds, and deep honey-colored wood floors.

Ming is inspired by Bombay's Chinese restaurants and combines Indian spices and ingredients with influences from China and Southeast Asia. Typical dishes include spicy coriander soup, eggplant with paneer cheese in spicy hoisin sauce, roasted sliced chili duck cooked Hakka-style, and braised sliced lamb. A giant Buddha, Chinese watercolors, and bright flowers greet customers at the entrance, and inside there are both wood and clear glass tables—with goldfish in tanks below the glass.

Back on the lower level, Mithaas is a Starbucks-meets-Bollywood dessert, tea, and snack shop featuring glass case after glass case of shimmering jewel-like Indian sweets, many enrobed in silver foil. Next door is the Mirage catering hall, and a short drive along Oak Tree Road is Moghul Express, which serves an amalgam of foods from the other Mehtani operations in a casual, stand-at-a-counter-and-eat environment: everything from South Indian to Chinese to Thai to desserts to party platters is on offer. In a shrinking world, this may be the menu of the future.

After touring the Mehtani empire in Edison, where the family is local royalty, greeted by name by shopkeepers, pedestrians, and cops, Shaun Mehtani takes me to the site of his three new restaurant projects about thirty-five miles north, in Morristown. I follow him along New Jersey's highways at police-chase speeds and we park underground at the Morristown Hyatt. Shaun is overseeing the renovation of a huge chunk of the Hyatt's street-level atrium, where there will soon be three restaurants arrayed in a hub-and-spokes configuration around a shared vestibule and with an interconnected kitchen facility.

Mendhi is an updated version of Moghul, with similar cuisine but a more sumptuous, luxurious look and feel, including twenty-three Fortuny chandeliers and art by San Francisco's Brian Schmierer. Ming II, the Morristown outpost of Ming, has as its central architectural feature an arched wood-slat ceiling. Shaun's personal favorite, however, is SM23 (named for his initials and birthday). SM23 is a contemporary cocktail lounge modeled after Pegu Club, Death & Co., and Milk & Honey in New York City. International cocktail star Grant Collins, of Australia-based Bar Solutions, designed the cocktail menu and made several trips from Down Under to train the SM23 staff.

Opening night, it's Shaun's twenty-third birthday, and all three Morristown venues are debuting at once. Hundreds of friends, family, and local media crowd the three restaurants. So ravenous are the assembled masses that the kitchen can barely keep up with this trial by fire, but as the evening wears on and appetites are satisfied, the dancing begins. Shaun and his mother, now sixty, dance until the wee hours.

A few weeks later, the kitchens are up to speed and all three restaurants are full at 6 P.M. We start with cocktails and appetizers at SM23, have entrees at Ming II, more entrees and desserts at Mendhi (where we get henna tattoos from the restaurant's on-call Mendhi artist), and then return to SM23 for more cocktails. Shaun, who normally works twelve-hour days but is up to more like sixteen hours since the opening, never slows in pace or conversation.

As Shaun drives me home in his BMW (he lives in Manhattan, where he recently graduated from NYU's Stern School of Business), listening to Indian dance music from his iPod connected to the car stereo, I mention how impressive it is that his new restaurants are full and functioning so well so soon. He replies, perhaps foreshadowing a Mehtani restaurant once again gracing New York City, "It's a start."

Indian Cuisine in the West: The commonwealth of kebabs and the curious case of curry

The Mehtanis and their restaurant group are atypical for many reasons, including the leadership of a female entrepreneur and the significant responsibilities given to a twenty-three-year-old son. But perhaps the most atypical thing about the Mehtanis is that they're Indian. Most Indian restaurants in the West—almost 95 percent—are owned by people from Bangladesh.

Like most Americans, I had only a dim awareness of Bangladesh. That is, it was dim until my wife, while flying to Nepal, got rerouted to Bangladesh because of mechanical difficulties with the plane. When she called me from the airport to report this turn of events, it prompted me to take a closer look at the map of South Asia.

India, Pakistan, and Bangladesh fit together as if they're part of one country, and indeed they used to be. (Nepal, which also fits neatly into that geographic jigsaw puzzle, lost some territory to India but was always independent). When the British returned India to local rule in 1947, they partitioned the area into two countries: India and Pakistan. Pakistan was not a contiguous nation. To the northwest of India lay West Pakistan, and to the northeast lay East Pakistan. Later, in the early 1970s, East Pakistan ceded from West Pakistan and became Bangladesh. Because Pakistan was a Muslim-majority country and India had a Hindu majority, millions of people migrated north or south (and many died) in order to avoid being in a religious minority. So while the countries are very different today, they share a common history. If all three were recombined into one country, it would have a larger population than China.

MANY PEOPLE, WHEN THEY think of British cuisine, think of dishes like fish and chips, bubble and squeak, and toad-in-the-hole. But the most popular dish in Great Britain today is curry. Anglicized Indian curries, the hearty stews of meat, vegetables, and blends of Indian spices, have become so thoroughly enmeshed in the culture that most Brits think of curry as a traditional British food, the way Americans think of pizza. At this point, it is.

British rule in India reached its peak in the late nineteenth century, and many British citizens spent time in India for military, governmental, or business purposes. Indian restaurants became a part of the fabric of London at that time, and England's curry culture began in earnest. In the twentieth century, many South Asians from India, Pakistan, and Bangladesh came to London to find work, leading to a boom in Indian cuisine, especially in the Brick Lane neighborhood. The popular dish "chicken tikka masala" was developed in the 1960s by Brick Lane restaurants looking to cater to local tastes. Along with curry, chicken tikka masala is to this day one of the most popular Indian dishes in the West, even though it is not part of traditional Indian cuisine.

Anglo-Indian cuisine made the jump to North America starting with the 1965 Immigration Act and accelerating in the 1970s, when immigration to England started to decline. Bangladeshi immigrants, in particu-

lar, adopted the Anglo-Indian formula and opened restaurants around the United States, especially in New
York City, Washington, D.C., San Francisco, Los Angeles, Chicago, and Edison, New Jersey. South Asian immigration to Canada picked up around the same time,
and Toronto and Vancouver developed particularly rich
Indian-cuisine scenes.

There is some irony in the prevalence of Bangladeshi
chefs and restaurateurs in the Indian culinary culture of
the West. The food served in the typical North American
or British Indian restaurant derives largely from the rich
Moghul cuisine of northern India. This is not what Bangladeshis eat. Rather, it is what they reckoned Westerners
would enjoy eating. Thus, while there are thousands of Indian restaurants owned and operated by Bangladeshi (as
well as a fair number of Pakistani) restaurateurs and chefs
in North America, there are very few Bangladeshi (or Pakistani) restaurants. It's as though hundreds of thousands of
Mexicans moved to China and opened New York–style
delis, never revealing that at home they eat tacos rather
than pastrami.

In the past couple of decades, this has begun to
change. As Western palates have become more adven-
turesome, Bangladeshi and Pakistani restaurateurs have
started including some of the dishes of their native cuisines on their menus. Pakistani and Afghani kebabs have
been especially successful, giving rise to a number of
restaurants dedicated only to that food. In addition,
dishes from the other regions of India, particularly the
East and South Indian regions (which themselves include many subregions), have been gaining a bit of popularity, and a few dedicated South Indian restaurants
now exist.

THE SOFT BIGOTRY OF LOW PRICE EXPECTATIONS

What is an "ethnic" restaurant? The term is widely used in conversation but is not well defined. After all, everybody has an ethnicity. Yet not all food is considered ethnic.

In a country like India, where the national and regional cuisines are well established, it's easy to say what's ethnic: a Chinese restaurant, a pizzeria, and a taco shop would all be ethnic from the Indian perspective. But in North America, there really isn't a native culinary culture—there are no Iroquois restaurants listed in the Zagat survey, and the standard menu served at most diners is not exactly a full-blown cuisine. The dominant cuisine in North America is an amalgam of dishes and influences from around the world, with local adaptations.

To some extent, in North America "ethnic" also means "not white" to many people. But upon examination that assumption falls apart: nobody considers African-American foods like southern fried chicken to be ethnic, and there are many ethnic groups—Jewish, Italian—that are Caucasian.

So when people say "ethnic," what they really mean is "other." It's a matter of perspective: growing up in New York City, whether you're Jewish, black, or WASP, you probably wouldn't consider Jewish food to be ethnic. But growing up in Utah, you might. And the definition of "other" changes over time. Fifty years ago, most North Americans would have considered Italian food to be ethnic. Today Italian food is as much a part of the mainstream as the hamburger.

But people also mean something else when they say "ethnic." They mean "cheap." If somebody suggests, "Let's have ethnic tonight," it's not likely to be interpreted to include the expensive French restaurant downtown. "Ethnic" is code for "cheap." And "cheap" has come to define "ethnic."

The great cuisines of Asia have histories stretching back thousands of years, through generations of royal courts and culinary ingenuity. Yet Americans balk at paying more than $8.95 for an entree in a Chinese restaurant. People think nothing of paying in the high $20s for steak or seafood in American restaurants (more in the large cities, where $30 to $40 entrees are common), even though the preparation of that kind of food requires little skill and could easily be done at home by the average cook. Meanwhile, the local Asian restaurant is serving labor-intensive, interesting, international food that would be difficult to produce at home, and consumers expect it to be inexpensive.

The cheapness of Asian cuisines has been a blessing and a curse. It has allowed those cuisines to rise in popularity, but it has also created a glass ceiling. Asian restaurants in North America are already good and getting better, but the way they'll become truly great is for consumers to be willing to pay steakhouse prices for Asian food. Imagine what those same efficient, resourceful, tireless Asian chefs could do with a $30 entree. The double standard makes little sense.

The good news is that the general bias toward cheap Asian food presents opportunities for those who are willing to pay more. And not a lot more, either. The difference in prices between the best and worst Indian restaurant in a given town may be just a few dollars, but those few dollars may buy a totally different level of cuisine. Countless times when researching this book, I saw some customers at a given Asian restaurant—be it Chinese, Japanese, Indian, or any other type—eating better than the others. Most serious Asian restaurants have good stuff in reserve that they'll be happy to sell you: limited quantities of better seafood, interesting imported produce, unusual sauces and condiments. You just have to express a willingness to experiment, and to pay a few dollars more.

Inside Indian Restaurants

The standard Indian-restaurant menu in North America consists mostly of dishes from northern India, especially Moghul dishes, combined with hybrid and adapted dishes developed in the United Kingdom and the United States to appeal to Western palates. While this menu defines what many people consider to be the scope of Indian cuisine, it's only the beginning. However, because so many Indian restaurants in the West follow this basic formula, it's best to become conversant with it.

Before dissecting the standard Indian menu, however, here are five tips for getting the most out of any Indian restaurant. In addition, many of the tips in the other chapters of this book apply equally to Indian restaurants.

Look Beyond the Buffet

Unlike most Chinese buffets, where the entire restaurant is conceived and implemented as a buffet-only operation, Indian restaurants often offer a choice: you can order from the menu, or you can eat from the buffet. The buffet does have some advantages: you can try many dishes, and the price is likely to be relatively low. But if it's quality you're after, you should do what educated Indian customers do: order from the menu. Your food will be made fresh to order, you'll be able to choose exactly what you want, and the restaurant's staff will recognize you as the connoisseur you are.

Order Made-to-Order Dishes

Just ordering from the menu instead of choosing the buffet isn't enough; you also have to choose wisely. While curries and other stewlike dishes are by far the most popular selections at Indian restaurants in North America, other dishes are often the better choices. Those stewlike dishes are often made, entirely or partly, in advance and lack the vibrant freshness of truly great Indian cooking. Instead, it's best to focus on items that are necessarily cooked to order. Tandoor-cooked items, in particular, are great choices. Even a mediocre Indian restaurant can usually produce an array of delicious cooked-to-order breads from the tandoor, and tandoor-cooked meats are one of my favorite foods. You may, however, need to insist on having your tandoori meats cooked to order, because some restaurants precook them and just heat them up in the tandoor.

Find Out Who Owns the Restaurant

Most Indian restaurants are not owned by Indians, and even the ones that are Indian-owned are likely to serve northern Indian cuisine, no matter what part of India the owners are from. It's well worth finding out where the owners and chefs are actually from, because in many cases there are a few dishes on the menu that come from outside the standard repertoire and reflect the cuisine of the owners' home territory. I was recently in an Indian restaurant that had a 95-percent standard menu, with just a few dishes marked "(East Indian)" next to their descriptions. I asked, and sure enough the chef and owner were from that part of India. Guess which dishes were the best, most flavorful, most carefully made offerings at the restaurant?

Be Willing to Pay More for Quality

In Indian restaurants, as in many things, you often get what you pay for. There are some places that are rip-offs, where you pay higher prices for atmospherics but don't actually get better food. But for the most part, a more expensive Indian restaurant will offer superior ingredients and more interesting dishes. So while it's tempting to choose the cheapest curry in town, it's often worth a few dollars more to have the best.

Look for Nonformulaic Restaurants with Personality

Some restaurants do the standard Indian-restaurant menu better than others. Some do it very well indeed.

But chances are it's the nonstandard, nonformulaic restaurants that will have the best and most interesting food. For example, if you're lucky enough to have access to a kebab-only restaurant (which will likely be Pakistani-owned), it will probably have superior kebabs to the surrounding general-menu Indian restaurants. The same holds true for regional Indian specialists and even Indian vegetarian restaurants—they're well worth trying.

BEGINNER: BASIC INDIAN-RESTAURANT DISHES

A typical Indian restaurant menu is divided into appetizers, meat entrees, seafood entrees, clay oven–cooked (tandoori) items, vegetables, and breads. If you dine at an Indian buffet, chances are the buffet will be balanced among these types of food as well. The following are the most popular and typical Indian-restaurant menu items I've seen when dining around North America.

Appetizers

Samosas. These Indian snacks are popular around the world, from Brazil to West Africa. A typical samosa is triangular in shape and consists of a pastry crust surrounding a filling that can be potato, meat, fish, or just about anything else (there are even sweet samosas). Most restaurants offer a couple of choices. Half the fun of eating samosas is dipping them in the chutneys that accompany them. Most often you'll see sweet tamarind chutney, refreshing mint chutney, and spicy onion chutney on the table. Be sure not to overlook them.

Pakoras. Another popular Indian street-food snack that serves as an appetizer in Western restaurants, pakoras are fried vegetable fritters. Many restaurants offer a choice of spinach (*palak*) pakoras or curd cheese (*paneer*) pakoras. Like samosas, they're also meant to be dipped in chutney.

Mulligatawny soup. An Anglo-Indian invention, the word *mulligatawny* literally means "pepper water," but pepper is not actually a major flavor in the soup. There are as many mulligatawny-soup recipes as there are restaurants that serve it, and there are no real rules. In North America the soup is likely to be prepared with lentils, tomatoes, and curry-like spices in a creamy broth.

Meat Entrees

Curry dishes. Contrary to popular belief, curry is not a specific spice, nor a specific dish.

THE GREAT CURRY CAPER

The last time I was at Sinha Trading, my favorite Indian spice shop (it's on Lexington Avenue in one of Manhattan's two Little India neighborhoods), I counted more than a hundred different spices on offer, everything from the common (turmeric, coriander) to the precise (a dozen different varieties of peppercorns) to the weird (myrobalan chabulic, which is said to cure constipation). There's one spice that you won't find at Sinha Trading, though, and that's a spice called "curry." The reason: there's no such thing.

Curry is perhaps the greatest misnomer in the history of cuisine. Not only is there no spice called curry, there's also no usable definition beyond "something with spices in it." The term is used to refer to so many disparate dishes and spice combinations that it has little real meaning—it's so inclusive that it barely excludes anything.

You'll find dishes called curries everywhere from India, to Southeast Asia, to Japan, to the United Kingdom, and they will taste nothing like one another. You'll find powders and pastes labeled "curry" at markets the world over, but there's no standard formula. In the West, most curry powder is based on turmeric, cumin, coriander, and pepper, whereas a Thai curry paste could be built around lemongrass, garlic, fish sauce, nutmeg, cinnamon, cumin, coriander, and coconut milk. A Japanese curry *(kare)* might be a thick brown sauce spooned over a deep-fried pork cutlet *(katsu kare)*, while a Cambodian curry *(kari)* could be a light, white, delicately seasoned sauce used for steaming fish (as in the dish *amok)*, and a British curry (like vindaloo) is a heavy, wicked stew of meat and vegetables. Save for the overlap of a spice here and there, they taste nothing alike.

This is all further complicated by the existence of a tree called the curry tree, which produces curry leaves. If you grind up curry leaves, however, you don't get curry powder. Curry leaves are more like a South Asian version of the bay leaf, used as an aromatic in simmered dishes.

So the next time somebody tries to sell you curry, be sure to ask questions. You never know what branch of the curry tree you're barking up.

Inferior restaurants use premixed curry powders like the ones sold at supermarkets, but the better Indian restaurants make their own spice blends in several varieties appropriate to different dishes. The standard North Indian–restaurant curry dish is a thick, spicy stew of meat and vegetables, usually offered with beef, lamb, or chicken (seafood is less common). The customer can specify the level of spice, and the hottest curry is often listed separately as "vindaloo." Another common option is *kofta* curry, which is made with lamb or chicken meatballs instead of chunks of meat.

Tandoori dishes. Yogurt-marinated skewers of chicken, lamb, shrimp, or vegetables are roasted in the searing-hot tandoor oven. The popular dish "chicken tikka masala" consists of tandoor-roasted chicken that is then sautéed with clarified butter (ghee), cream, and spices.

Kebabs. Using a technique similar to tandoori dishes but with a different flavor profile, kebabs are not marinated in yogurt but rather in bright seasonings like vinegar, ginger, and pepper. Kebabs come as solid chunks of meat, or as balls of various seasoned ground meats.

Breads

Naan (often written "nan"). Unleavened bread baked in the tandoor, usually spread with butter. Variants of naan include garlic naan (the naan equivalent of garlic bread), Peshwari naan (naan stuffed with dried fruits and nuts), and onion *kulcha* (naan stuffed with seasoned onion).

Paratha. Layers of bread, spread with clarified butter (ghee) and baked in the tandoor. Paratha variants include *alu paratha* (stuffed with potatoes), *keema paratha* (stuffed with chopped meat); and *Muglai paratha* (stuffed with egg and chopped meat).

Roti. Round whole-wheat bread baked in the tandoor.

Puri. Whole-wheat-flour puffed bread, deep-fried.

TALES OF THE TANDOOR

It seems that every culture with a cuisine has invented one or another way of applying extreme heat to food. The tandoor, however, is perhaps the simplest and most elegant, effective, and screamingly hot of all. It's essentially a huge clay pot with an opening at the top and an exhaust vent at the bottom. The chamber is surrounded by wood coals, and the internal temperature achieves a steady, bone-dry heat in the 800° to 900°F range. Modern restaurant tandoors are gas-fired and constructed of various high-tech ceramics, but the fundamental principles are the same. The tandoor probably originated in the area now known as Afghanistan and came south to India with the Moghuls.

Unlike a Western bread oven, where you put bread on the oven's floor and let it sit there to cook, the tandoor has a hole in the bottom. So you cook the bread on the side. It seems counterintuitive, cooking bread on the oven wall, but it works. Indian flatbreads, like naan, are formed as disks and then literally slapped on the wall of the tandoor, where they stick for a few minutes, held in place by seemingly magical forces, until they're removed.

I had long been intrigued by tandoori ovens and wanted to try my hand at making bread in one, but I never guessed it would happen for me in Winnipeg.

At the East India Company, owned by Kamal Mehra and his wife, Sudha, I was welcomed into the kitchen of Winnipeg's premier Indian restaurant. As I do whenever I manage to get into an Indian-restaurant kitchen, I gravitated to the tandoor and gawked like a little boy at a construction site. Eventually, unable to move me off my spot, their son and my guide, Sachit, asked me, "Would you like to try it?"

I donned a hairnet (my wife to this day occasionally blackmails me with threats of releasing the photographs) and was given a brief safety lecture. "You see that guy with one eye? That's what happens when you're not careful around the tandoor." I couldn't tell if it was a joke or not. I confronted the tandoor, staring into its gaping maw, so hot I could see the air rippling around the opening. I contemplated whether the experience would be worth the risk to my eye. I decided to move forward.

The tandoor chef (most Indian restaurants have a chef devoted entirely to cooking in the tandoor) showed me the procedure for putting a piece of naan in the tandoor: he placed the disk of flatbread dough on a small pillow-like pad made of heatproof fabric ("for a few seconds, it's heatproof, at least," explained Sachit), then with a smooth motion and a decisive arc of his arm, he swooped down, slapped the bread against the wall of the tandoor, and got his hand and the pillow out of there.

My motion wasn't nearly as smooth. First, I hung my hand over the opening for so long (like, four seconds) that even though my hand was at least a foot from the tandoor, I couldn't keep it there anymore and had to give up. On my second attempt, I didn't make a decisive enough move toward the wall, and my unleavened, uncooked naan fell to the bottom, where it had to be extracted with tongs by the disappointed tandoor chef. But on my third try, it all came together. I kept my eyes open, I made a decisive movement, and my naan actually stuck to the wall. There it sat, cooking, while I stared at it. Finally I was shoved aside by the now-bored tandoor cook, who removed the finished bread, brushed it with clarified butter, and let me eat it since it was too ugly to serve to paying customers.

Naan is one of the most delicious breads in the world, and it's hard to stop eating it. I know. I've eaten so much at a sitting that I felt like a goldfish (domestic goldfish, left to their own devices, would eat until they explode). The tandoor, however, is not just for bread. Skewered meats, often marinated in yogurt-based sauces, are placed in the tandoor in order to sear and roast them quickly so they get crisp on the outside but stay moist on the inside.

Nor are Indian foods the only things cooked in the tandoor. After hours, at many Indian restaurants the cooks put all sorts of things into the tandoor for their own meals: hot dogs, hot pockets, potatoes, even skewered steaks. They all cook beautifully.

At the end of my visit to the East India Company,

Sachit presented me with a precious bagful of his family's garam masala, the signature spice blend responsible for the flavor of many of the restaurant's dishes. I accepted it gratefully. However, I felt compelled to discard it before crossing the border. The last thing I needed to do was have to explain to the border patrol why I had a paper bag filled with greenish-brown powder in the back seat.

INTERMEDIATE: MOVING BEYOND THE BASICS TO SEAFOOD, RICE, AND VEGETABLE DISHES

The basic dishes described above comprise the overwhelming majority of orders in Indian restaurants in North America, but some of the best items on the menu can be found outside the typical categories. India is virtually surrounded by water, and seafood is a significant part of the diet there, so Indian seafood dishes are often an untapped vein of deliciousness. With most Indian restaurants owned by Bangladeshis, and with seafood such a major part of Bangladeshi cuisine due to its long coastline and major rivers, chances are the chefs really know how to cook seafood. In addition, India is home to the world's largest population of vegetarians. Rice dishes in Indian cuisine are diverse and should be thought of as more than just side dishes.

Seafood Dishes

Pomfret. The fish we call pompano in the West is what Indians call pomfret. However, when Indians speak of the dish "pomfret," they imply more than just the type of fish. My friend Monica Bhide, the Indian cookbook author, has written so lovingly of pomfret that I order it almost every chance I get. Pomfret is served as a whole fish, stuffed with tamarind and mango, fried, and served in a coconut curry sauce. You may also see pomfret on the menus of Southeast Asian restaurants, as the preparation has migrated to those cultures as well.

Dopeaja. This is fish cooked with scallions, tomatoes, and spices including chilies, turmeric, ginger, and pepper. Usually made with chunks of fish, on menus dopeaja will usually be modified by the type of fish, for example *tilapia dopeaja*. Shrimp are also sometimes offered, in which case they'll be whole shrimp, not chunks.

Mustard fish. The traditional East Indian preparation uses a fish called *hilsa*. In the West, most any whitefish, such as chunks of cod, may be used, and it's also sometimes made with salmon. Ground mustard seeds, chilies, and spices are simmered with the fish into a heady stew with a pronounced (though not bitter, if made well) mustardy flavor.

Fish kofta curry (pholly). Although most people think of curries as meat dishes, one of my favorite curry dishes is made with fish. The fish balls in fish kofta curry are essentially lightly spiced meatballs made from fish rather than meat. Fish kofta curry is typically mild as curries go, so as not to overwhelm the fish.

Rice and Vegetable Dishes

Biryani. Like curry, *biryani* is a generic term that encompasses countless dishes. Biryanis are popular all over India and reflect the Persian influence on Indian cuisine. The word itself just means "fried." In most Indian restaurants in the West, the standard biryani preparation is the Bangla-deshi one, which consists of beef, lamb, chicken, fish, shrimp, or vegetables cooked with saffron rice and spices. Watch for interesting regional variants as well, such as Hyderabadi biryani. (Because it's Persian in derivation, don't be surprised if you see biryani on menus in Middle Eastern restaurants as well.)

Indian vegetarian cuisine. While Indian cuisine as served in the West tends to be meat-heavy, the vegetarian population of India is huge. Most estimates place the number of Indian vegetarians at around the same as the entire population of the United States: somewhere in the neighborhood of 300 million people. As a result, Indian vegetarian cuisine is perhaps the world's most highly developed: unlike the health-food-oriented vegetarian food that pervades North

CLEANLINESS

Every Asian-restaurant kitchen in North America is subject to the same health codes as all other restaurant kitchens, yet there is a widely held belief among the restaurant-going public that Asian-restaurant kitchens are unclean. This stereotype, repeated endlessly online (one of the most persistent urban legends is that Asian restaurants use the meat of stray cats) and either stated or lurking just below the surface, is simply false.

There are, to be sure, some filthy Asian restaurants out there, just as there are plenty of filthy burger joints, pizzerias, taco shops, and fancy

French restaurants. But I've visited nearly a hundred restaurant kitchens in the course of researching my books and articles and have never observed a pattern of poor sanitation unique to Asian restaurants. Nor do health inspection scores, available to the public online for many cities, support any claim of Asian restaurants being held to a lower standard of compliance.

Anyone concerned about food safety is better off avoiding raw vegetables than Asian restaurants. The most significant food safety issues of recent times have involved vegetables eaten raw. The excrement of cows, sheep, and pigs can contaminate food at its source with E. coli, as was recently believed to be the case with California spinach and with vegetables served at Taco Bell.

If people really wanted to be safe, they'd cook everything in a wok. Woks, which are used all over Asia (in India they're called *karahi*), often reach sustained temperatures higher than any Western-style pot because they have special burners. The British thermal unit (BTU) is the measure of energy output used to describe stoves. A typical home range's burners produce 12,000 BTUs per hour. A professional restaurant stove, such as you'd find in a Western restaurant kitchen, might produce 24,000 BTUs per hour. A professional restaurant wok burner, by contrast, has twenty or more gas jets producing a combined total of 125,000 or more BTUs per hour. Some wok burners are so powerful that their gas jets are built out of stone, because metal just wouldn't be up to the task. When stir-frying, the ingredients must be kept in constant motion. If they come to rest for even a few seconds, they'll burn. Asian dishes that aren't cooked at super-high temperatures, such as curries, are often stewed for long periods of time, a method that equally neutralizes potentially harmful bacteria.

What, then, explains the stereotype of the unclean Asian restaurant?

Perhaps it's a hasty generalization based on a few dirty restaurants. Perhaps it's the smell of fish that's apparent when walking through many Chinatowns in North America—alarming to many Westerners, so removed from the food supply that they've become accustomed to everything being shrink-wrapped, sealed, and displayed in refrigerated cases. But most likely it's a thinly veiled form of xenophobia, a reaction to differences in people and food manifesting itself as a belief that they're unclean.

America, good Indian vegetarian cuisine doesn't leave one longing for meat. In some cities with larger Indian immigrant populations, you might find entire vegetarian Indian restaurants (one such restaurant near me, Dimple, is vegetarian and kosher, and has an amazing vegetarian buffet that changes daily and allows you to try a dozen different vegetarian items at a time). But even standard Indian restaurants tend to have many vegetable offerings. Look for *chana masala* (spiced chickpeas), *palak paneer* (curd cheese cooked with spinach, seasonings, and spices), *alu ghobie bhajee* (cauliflower and potatoes), *navratna korma* (mixed vegetables in yogurt sauce), *aam dal angon* (lentils cooked with mango and spices), *malai kofta* (potato and cheese balls), *bendi masala* (chopped okra cooked with spices, tomato, and onion), *paneer makhani* (spiced cheese in a creamy sauce), *begun bharta* (eggplant baked, mashed, and seasoned with herbs and spices), *alu bharta* (potato baked, mashed, mixed with fried onions, and seasoned with herbs and spices), and the condiment *raita* (fresh yogurt with diced cucumber and spices).

ADVANCED: SOUTH INDIAN CUISINE

If you've ever called for tech support, chances are you've spoken to an operator in Bangalore, the central city of South India (its population is nearly 7 million) and the capital of the state of Karnataka. South India has produced so many engineers and scientists that it's nearly impossible to set foot in a technology or pharmaceutical company anywhere in the world without running into several South Indians. So successful has the region been at building its technology economy that recently Bangalore companies have been outsourcing some of their technology work to the West. South India, however, has not been as successful at exporting its cuisine. Most South Indians in the West aren't interested in the restaurant business, and the Bangladeshi restaurant community has been slow to incorporate South Indian dishes.

Still, although northern Indian cuisine and the standard menu that has grown out of it have dominated the Indian-restaurant scene in the West for decades, the cuisine of southern India has been gradually rising in popularity.

Southern Indian cuisine comes from the states of Andhra Pradesh, Tamil Nadu, Karnataka, and Kerala, and is more oriented toward rice, vegetables, and fish than is northern Indian cuisine.

My guide to the cuisine of South India for the past year has been Danashekar Subbiah—his nickname is, mercifully, "Shekar"—who manages the restaurant Moksha in Edison, New Jersey, where his wife was the opening chef

TIPPED OFF

Tipping is often the cause of much consternation among restaurant-goers in North America. In talking to people about Asian restaurants, I've often been asked how much to tip at a buffet; how much to tip for delivery; whether to tip on carry-out orders; and whether "normal" restaurant-tipping percentages apply in Asian restaurants.

There are simple answers to these questions: Tip 15 percent at a buffet or for delivery (it's not a lot: $1.50 per person at a $10-per-person buffet). Tipping is not expected on carry-out orders, but a couple of dollars will always be appreciated. And yes, when dining in an Asian restaurant one should tip the same 16 to 20 percent as at any restaurant—and more for truly exceptional service.

Yet, while it's easy enough to say how much to tip, the issue of tipping is complex and raises fundamental questions about the workings of the restaurant business and the economy. It seems that everybody—customers, servers, and restaurant owners—supports the tipping system. But it's worth exploring why it might be wrong to stick with the practice.

Customers believe in tipping because they think it makes economic sense. "Waiters know that they won't get paid if they don't do a good job" is how most advocates of the system would put it. To be sure, this is a seductive, seemingly rational statement about economic theory, but it appears to have little applicability to the real world of restaurants.

Michael Lynn, an associate professor of consumer behavior and marketing at Cornell's School of Hotel Administration, has conducted dozens of studies on tipping and has concluded that consumers' assessments of the quality of service correlate weakly to the amount they tip.

Rather, customers are likely to tip more in response to servers touching them lightly and crouching next to the table to make conversation than to how often their water glass is refilled—in other words, customers tip more when they like the server, not when the service is good. (Mr. Lynn's studies also indicate that male customers increase their tips for female servers while female customers increase their tips for male servers.)

What's more, consumers seem to forget that the tip increases as the bill increases. Thus, the tipping system is an open invitation to what restaurant professionals call "upselling": every bottle of beer, every extra appetizer, every dessert, is extra money in the server's pocket. Aggressive upselling and hustling for tips are often rewarded while low-key quality service often goes unrecognized.

In addition, the practice of tip pooling, which is becoming the norm in Asian restaurants as well as in Western fine-dining establishments—and, indeed, in just about every kind of restaurant above the level of a greasy spoon—has gutted whatever effect voting with your tip might have had on an individual waiter. In a perverse outcome, you are punishing the good waiters in the restaurant by not tipping the bad one. The pooling system is also subject to much abuse, as several recent lawsuits have demonstrated: the practice of managers and owners skimming off the tip pool is widespread, and recent immigrants (legal or not) are unlikely to have the resources to challenge the practice.

Waiters and waitresses also believe it is their right to be tipped. In most states, servers don't even get paid minimum wage by their employers. There is an exemption (called a "credit") for tipped employees that allows restaurants to pay them just a token couple of dollars an hour (as low as $1.59 per hour in Kansas and $3.85 per hour in New York City). They are instead largely paid by tips, to the tune of $26 billion per year.

When you talk to servers, you'll find that most believe they make more money under the tipping system than they would as salaried employees. And that's probably true, strictly speaking, assuming they're allowed to keep their tips. The tipping system makes waiters into something akin to independent contractors. And in almost any business the hourly wage of a contractor is higher than that of an employee. Yet in most businesses, people choose to be employees. That's because those who wish to guarantee their long-term financial security sacrifice a little bit of quick cash for longer-term benefits like health insurance, retirement plans, and vacation pay—a seemingly lofty goal for cheap ethnic restaurants, yet one that the history of immigration, assimilation, and advancement supports. But, of course, most servers see themselves as transient employees—waiting tables before moving on to bigger and better things.

Still, this may not always be the case. The large number of waiters I see in their forties, fifties, and sixties cast doubt on the theory. While kitchen workers trade low wages and no tips for a future in the business—the opportunity to rise in rank, to one day run a kitchen—what calculation do waiters and waitresses make? Under the tipping system, it seems, they're trading a little extra now for the promise of nothing later. There just might be a better way: almost every other kind of business in North America pays employees a salary and charges enough for goods and services to cover that salary. We don't tip our accountants or our high school principals because we assume they're paid enough to live—and we expect good service from them.

For their part, restaurateurs believe it is their right to have consumers pay servers, so they don't have to pay their employees a living wage. They prefer the current system because it allows them to have a team of pseudo-contractors rather than real employees. But that too is shortsighted. Over time, as in any service-oriented business, waiters loyal to the restaurant will perform better and make customers happier than waiters loyal only to themselves.

In this, the world's most generous nation of tippers, most restaurants don't even offer service as good as at the average McDonald's. While it lacks style, service at McDonald's is far more reliable than the service at the average upper-middle-market restaurant. This is not because the employees of McDonald's are brilliant at their jobs; it's because they're well trained and subject to rigorous supervision. And come to think of it, at McDonald's there is no tipping.

(she eventually trained her successors and went back to family life). Shekar and I have spoken at length about the challenges facing South Indian cuisine: with so few restaurants serving it, there is no standard menu, and there aren't five easily recognizable dishes that Western palates can rally around as a starting point. This is unfortunate, because with its eye toward healthfulness and balance, South Indian cuisine is well suited to modern tastes and ideas about eating. It deserves a larger audience in the West. As much as I love the cuisine of North India, it always tastes very heavy to me if I've recently had a South Indian meal.

The South Indian dish that has most thoroughly penetrated North America is the *dosa*. Sometimes even found on standard North Indian–restaurant menus, dosas (the plural is also sometimes written "dosai") are French-inspired crepes made of a slightly fermented batter of ground rice and yellow split peas, usually filled with vegetables or other vegetarian items; they are cooked on a griddle. There are several restaurants in the New York metro area with names like Dosa Hut that sell in the neighborhood of thirty kinds of dosas. Dosas can be thin and crisp or thick and soft. A related crepe called *idli* is made with steamed rice.

Because there's no standardized South Indian–restaurant menu in North America, you'll have to do a lot of improvising when you order. By now you should have the tools to improvise, interrogate, and invent without hesitation. You may even recognize commonalities with the other cuisines you've been mastering. For example, there are many linkages between South Indian and Southeast Asian cuisines—particularly the emphasis on fresh herbs and lighter preparation styles.

Banging the Drum for Indian Fusion

The morning of our son PJ's second birthday, I asked him what he'd like for dinner. His answer: "Naan!"

"Naan," in PJ-speak, is shorthand for his favorite restaurant: Tabla, a cutting-edge Indian restaurant in New York City. Though naan is just one of many items on Tabla's two menus, it's PJ's priority item and he has therefore decided to call the whole restaurant "Naan!" So excited was PJ about his birthday dinner at Tabla that he skipped his nap.

In 1998 the chef Floyd Cardoz and the restaurateur Danny Meyer (who also operates the famed Union Square Café and Gramercy Tavern) quietly unleashed Tabla on the New York restaurant scene. I don't think anybody— even those who, like me, loved the place from the start— predicted that it would become one of the world's most important Indian restaurants. Even today, Tabla's significance is not widely appreciated outside a small community of globally aware Indian chefs.

Tabla (named for a kind of Indian drum) always felt like a whimsical, almost accidental place, especially to those familiar with the backstory: Tabla was something of an unintended consequence of historic preservation. The wall dividing the ground-floor space in the Metropolitan Life building, an Art Deco landmark on Madison Square Park, left a niche just large enough, after the mega-project of Eleven Madison Park (which was supposed to be the splashier of the two restaurants) was conceived, for a boutique restaurant sporting a seemingly whimsical concept: "Indian fusion."

Today what was once called Indian fusion has acquired what I think is a more appropriate moniker: New Indian cooking. What was once iconoclastic is now one of the most significant movements in modern cuisine. And Tabla is at its nexus.

The Asian fusion trend reached its apex in the 1990s, but India has long held the pole position when it comes to the mastery of spices. Even the Southeast Asian cuisines, which utilize spices to such great effect, ultimately look to India as the progenitor of curries and other complex spice blends. And spices represent, to me, the most neglected frontier of Western cuisine. New Indian cooking, though not as sizable a movement as Asian fusion, is not only about Indian cuisine, and not only about the effect of

Western technique and ingredients on that cuisine, but also about what India has to teach Western chefs about an entire category of flavors. I think that in the final analysis, the West will learn as much or more from India as from the rest of Asia.

As Tabla was making its presence felt and slowly working through its early dysfunction over its self-perception ("Are we an Indian restaurant or what?"), its perception in the Indian community ("It's not Indian enough!"), and its perception in the Western culinary community ("It's too Indian!"), there were other restaurants throughout North America working independently toward a common goal. In Vancouver, Vikram Vij was operating the renowned Vij's, which I've been calling the best Indian restaurant in North America for almost a decade. In Boston, Thomas John was developing the message at Mantra. More recently, in New York, the team of Suvir Saran and Hemant Mathur have been introducing a new level of rigor to Indian cuisine, first at Diwan, then at Amma, then at Dévi. And Madhur Jaffrey, the polymath actress, chef, and super-genius, has been laying the foundations of New Indian cooking since the rest of these guys were in diapers.

Which brings us to a special dinner commemorating Tabla's birthday, when all the aforementioned chefs came together to demonstrate where New Indian cooking is today.

There were some delicious dishes served that night. Suvir Saran and Hemant Mathur were given the task of awakening guests' palates with a series of hors d'oeuvres that included a bracing shrimp rasam (soup) with buttermilk and little florets of Manchurian cauliflower (we all need this recipe). They were also responsible for continuing the momentum through the first course: "sprouted beans chat, crispy spinach millefeuille." It was a remarkable dish, the crisped leaves of spinach serving as the layers in a savory postmodern Indian take on the traditional French pastry.

This gave way to Madhur Jaffrey's jumbo shrimp in a sauce featuring fennel seeds, mustard seeds, and curry leaves. I don't think there's a word for the color of this sauce, which fell somewhere between peach melba and coral, but in honor of it I'd like to paint my whole house that shade. I asked her if I could have a gallon and she laughed, thinking I wasn't serious.

Thomas John, for his part, offered caramelized red snapper with spiced yucca, accompanied by the most vibrant salad of fava beans and watermelon. Jaffrey is a tough act to follow, but John's little bits of watermelon managed to penetrate the fog that her haunting sauce had left over the audience.

Floyd Cardoz countered with crispy spice-crusted soft-shell crabs over a medley of pickled ramps, long squash, bacon, and crab curry. Luckily I was seated next to a non-soft-shell eater so I got to eat two portions.

Finally, like an invading army, Vikram Vij's ghee-braised short ribs (pause to consider that: short ribs braised in clarified butter!) with cinnamon and red wine curry flattened the terrain.

I can't imagine being a pastry chef in this situation, playing to an exhausted house that has had its palate collectively pounded on by the entire flavor range of the Penzeys spice catalog, but Jehangir Mehta, the pastry chef at the restaurant Aix, served up one of the best desserts I've had in ages: a salty caramel tapioca tart with pomegranate reduction, marinated mango, and citrus ice cream. The saltiness of this dessert was a stroke of genius, activating resources of flavor perception I thought I'd lost hours before. Sitting with my back to Tabla's central architectural feature, a giant hole in the second-story dining-room floor called "the oculus," I felt upon the first bite as though I might suddenly tumble backward through the hole and onto the stone floor below.

The overall meal experience was terrifically enjoyable and wildly synergistic. But what was far more significant to me was what it represented. Being at Tabla that night felt like being in a moment, one of those moments you know you'll return to time and again as history unfolds and gives us more perspective. There was a sense of being there while something important was happening. It could be seen on the chef's faces: what had been a fragmented community of kindred spirits, and had slowly developed into a movement, that night gelled into something more along the lines of a school of thought. And it was inspiring to see the audience, almost evenly divided between Indians and non-Indians, breaking bread together as a new gourmet community. It was quite a night, one I'll remember long after PJ has forgotten his second birthday.

SEARCHING FOR MOMO

Of all the dumplings of the world, momo are my favorite. Momo are popular among the peoples of the Himalayas (sandwiched between India and China) and have gained a toehold in the United

States, thanks to several restaurants opened by Tibetan and Nepalese refugees.

I first heard about them from my wife, Ellen, who has been to Nepal and Tibet half a dozen times. Every time we'd have dumplings in an Asian restaurant, be it Chinese, Japanese, or Korean, she'd declare, "These are good, but not as good as momo." The refrain became exhausting. Then one day in the early 1990s, a little Tibetan restaurant, Tibet Shambala, opened right across town from us. I would finally get to taste the legendary momo.

We entered the restaurant: a dark room with curtains drawn. We pushed aside some hanging beads and let our eyes adjust. Tibetan chants emanated from a portable stereo perched on a chair in the back corner, the walls were covered with posters featuring the Dalai Lama, and we were the only people in the room. Eventually a Tibetan woman wandered out (we later learned she was the wife of the owner, Norbu Tsering), seemed a bit surprised to see us, and took our order, which comprised every momo on the menu: *sha momo* (steamed dumplings stuffed with a mixture of ground beef, scallions, cilantro, and ginger), *tse momo* (steamed mixed vegetable dumplings), and *shogo fried momo* (stuffed with mashed potato and onion and pan-fried).

They were some of the best dumplings I'd ever had. Momo are more rustic than most Asian dumplings and are therefore looked down upon by many Asians as peasant food. But that's also their appeal: the simple flour-and-water dough, rolled thicker than in most Asian cuisines, forms a toothsome wrapper that holds a fat dollop of filling and can well withstand lengthy steaming, frying, or immersion in soup. The seasonings on the inside, plus the accompanying cilantro-laced hot red pepper sauce (so aggressive that it seemed out of character for Buddhist pacifists), make for an irresistible package. The menu at Tibet Shambala had many other offerings, but I made many a meal from a simple assemblage of momo.

The restaurant is long gone, but our love for the humble momo remains as strong as ever. We even named our bulldog Momo.

After Tibet Shambala closed, an unbearable drought set in. With no source nearby, we decided we had to learn how to make momo. Google was not particularly helpful, so Ellen contacted her friends Sonam Phuntsok and Tsering Choedon, a Tibetan refugee couple living in Queens (he drives a cab, she's a nanny), and asked for lessons. Moving at typical Tibetan Buddhist speeds, we first sat on the floor of their living room for a couple of hours, talking about the momo-making demonstration that was, at some point, going to happen. More Tibetans wandered in: Penpa Dolma (the grandmother), Tenzin (the daughter, named for the Dalai Lama), and assorted others who seemed neither to live there nor to be related. We had a glass of orange juice. As the exposition dragged on, I found myself anticipating the arrival of supporters of the Tibetan cause:

Laurie Anderson, maybe, or Phil Jackson. Richard Gere seemed like the very least I was entitled to expect.

Finally the group moved to the kitchen and an impromptu assembly line formed. Ellen was on dough-rolling duty. She took Ping-Pong-ball-size lumps of dough and flattened them into disks with a small wooden dowel. I was on momo-forming duty. Tsering showed me how to pinch the disks of dough around the filling in various designs. I got pretty good at making half-moons, was able to form the occasional successful beggar's purse, and couldn't even come close to mastering any of the more ambitious shapes. Tsering did a lot of repair work. We must have made 250 momo; I ate about 50. We took home a pint of freshly made hot sauce.

Despite the excellent instruction, we never quite mastered home momo-making. But just when I had resigned myself to a momo-less existence, we got a hot tip from Sonam. He was driving his cab around Jackson Heights, the neighborhood in Queens where there has been a recent influx of Nepalese and Tibetans, and he hit the momo jackpot.

As is typical in Asia, many of the stores have stores within stores. Sonam had directed us to an establishment on 74th Street (the main drag of Little India in Jackson Heights) that was an ostensible jewelry store. The jewelry store was not only selling jewelry but also leasing space to a luggage store, a tailor, and an AT&T cellular-phone store. Inside the AT&T store there was an area where one could buy

teapots and another area with a large collection of
DVDs of questionable copyright status. And there,
all the way in the back of the store, behind the
teapots, behind the cell phones, behind the videos,
was the momo counter. I felt as if we'd scaled
Everest—I was ready to plant the flag of the Momo
Nation.

It was closed. According to the salesman, they'd
had a plumbing problem and wouldn't be open again
for a couple of weeks. But he was sure he'd heard
about another nearby place selling momo—he just
couldn't remember any details. We set out to pinpoint
the wayward momo amid the swirling tumult of
Jackson Heights.

We had just about given up and were preparing to
settle for a dinner of Pakistani kebabs instead. But
as we trekked to the kebab place, Ellen noticed a
steep flight of metal steps leading down to a travel
agency called Himalaya Connection. There was
Tibetan writing on the sign. And I noticed, below
the Himalaya Connection sign, a paper sign that
said MOMO. We descended the stairs, went inside,
and found—in addition to the travel agency—an
astounding selection of Tibetan and Nepalese music
videos. But there was no sign of any momo. Upon
cross-examination, the travel agent revealed that the
MOMO signs were for another store, around the
corner and up a couple of blocks, where we were
assured there would be momo aplenty. He gave us
an address.

I was not feeling very Zen at this point and

wanted to give up. Even the irrepressible Dalai Lama would have been in despair, I'm certain. But Ellen, always the sherpa, insisted that we press on. Upon arrival, I was not optimistic. The place appeared to be an Internet cafe called Net Gen. Within the structure that promised to be an Internet cafe, however, was a makeshift restaurant: Cafe K-2. Of course.

They had momo. I ate many, and the balance of the universe was restored.

Conclusion

Ending the Tyranny of Authenticity: Accepting delicious developments

This book has been divided into sections focused on the cuisine of a country or area, with, in some cases, subsections focused on regional cuisines. These divisions and subdivisions are helpful from a practical standpoint: the human mind needs categories to make sense of things. But viewed from a higher altitude, the cuisines of Asia are an interconnected web of influences.

Take, for example, curry, which is seen in dishes across Asia, from the diverse curries of India, to variants in just about every Southeast Asian cuisine, to the katsu curry and curry rice of Japan. Likewise, one can follow a trail of dumplings from Korea's mandoo, to Japan's gyoza, to seemingly infinite dumpling varieties in China, to momo in Tibet and Nepal, to South Indian dumplings like kozhukattai and urundai kozambhu. Chopsticks in various modified forms are used, or have at some time been used, across most of Asia. Similar parallels can be drawn among Asian rice dishes, tofu dishes, tea rituals, wraps (Chinese moo shu and Peking duck pancakes, Korean ssam, Cambodian crepes, South Indian dosas), and more.

Viewed from a still higher altitude, the cuisines of the world display a startling degree of interconnectedness. For example, hot peppers, so integral to the cuisines of many Asian nations, are actually a food from the New World. Prior to Columbus's voyages, there were no hot peppers anywhere else, and they took centuries to migrate and become integral to Asian cuisine. Throughout this book, you've read numerous accounts of dishes and techniques migrating from one place to another, like Portuguese deep-frying as the progenitor of Japanese tempura. You may have noticed that I'm a bit of a dumpling addict, but I come by it honestly: dumplings are found not only in Asian cuisines but all over the world, as in the Eastern European dumplings called *pierogies* and *kreplach* that my ancestors ate. It's no surprise that a while back the winner of a pierogi-making competition held in New York was a Chinese-American woman.

Though I've eaten so much Chinese, Japanese, Korean, Indian, and Southeast Asian food that my Caucasian DNA could at any moment spontaneously resequence itself into Asian DNA, I've never spent much time in Asia. I've enjoyed the limited time I've spent there tremendously (though I can't say as much for the flight; my voluminous eating is evident in my bulk, which doesn't take well to twenty hours in an economy-class seat). I've spent enough time in Asia, however, to know that the food in any given Asian country can be quite different from its typical representation in restaurants in North America. Many of the dishes I enjoyed growing up, for example, are

Chinese-American creations: the obese Americanized egg rolls I love so much, General Tso's chicken, deep-fried egg foo yung with rich brown gravy.

It should hardly be surprising that as Asian cuisines have come to North America, they have adapted, evolved, and changed—just as they continue to adapt, evolve, and change back in Asia in response to contact with the West (one of the big culinary trends in Shanghai right now is the use of saffron).

It seems beyond obvious to state that cuisine is ever-evolving, yet you wouldn't necessarily pick that up from reading food magazines today. Instead, the word you're most likely to see used to describe a dish like General Tso's chicken is "inauthentic."

Reading the glossy food magazines, the newsletters, and the Internet, and even when talking to educated gourmets, I get the sense that the authenticity police are everywhere these days. Authenticity as commonly understood by today's reigning culinary authorities refers to the preservation of "original" recipes, presented with some historical and cultural context. In the language of *Merriam-Webster*, authentic means "conforming to an original so as to reproduce essential features."

But what if evolution itself lies at the core of authenticity? When hot chilies first appeared in China, did the local food cognoscenti protest, "We don't use these things in authentic Sichuan cuisine"? No cuisine springs into existence as a fully formed entity, and all living cuisines evolve. There was no tomato sauce—and there were certainly no sun-dried tomatoes—until centuries after the tomato first reached Europe from the New World. We could just as easily imagine knee-jerk authenticity-based complaints about chocolate in France and wine in Australia. If you dig really deep, you'll probably find that at some point in prehistory the very notion of cooking beasts over a fire—instead of eating their bloody haunches raw—was scorned for its inauthenticity, too.

Fusion—the mixing of cuisines from around the world—is not some trend that started in the 1980s. It is the very history of cuisine. No corner of Asia, from Japan to India, was untouched by the forced fusion of the Mongol empire, or by trade with the West.

Since everything in the world of food likely had some precursory experience, wouldn't it be smarter for us to make allowances for what "authentic" really means? If you ask me, such tolerance is necessary when you dine out in a place like the United States, where just about everybody came from somewhere else. Asian chefs, on arriving in North America, found different ingredients, faced different challenges, and adapted. They created new dishes and extended their native cuisines.

I believe these cooks demonstrate that authenticity isn't a repetition of history. Real authenticity, to me, is grounded in being faithful to oneself. This is the last definition given by *Merriam-Webster*, but to me it is the most appropriate for cuisine: "true to one's own personality, spirit, or character." That's why, despite their breaks with tradition, there's nothing inauthentic about egg rolls, or Japanese restaurants with far-ranging menus. Sometimes these concepts even get exported back to their parent cultures—for example with the opening of Nobu (a New York restaurant, based on a Los Angeles restaurant, serving Peruvian-influenced Japanese fusion cuisine) in Tokyo. Change for its own sake is phony, but true originality is authentic.

To me, what makes North America a supremely dynamic eating destination is exactly its unabashed dedication to what the old-school writers would call inauthenticity: the New World doesn't attempt to hide the actuality that human history is built on immigration, assimilation, and invention. Los Angeles is often referred to, here and in Asia, as Thailand's seventy-seventh province, and similar claims are made about other immigrant communities. The Asian communities of North America are as large as some entire nations, and they represent cultural and culinary evolution fully as robust as what's occurring back home. My memories of dining at Empire Szechuan would be utterly foreign to a resident of Sichaun province, but they're the authentic experiences of my American life.

Rather than obsessing about historical notions of authenticity, I propose finding culinary validation within ourselves and accepting that tomorrow's authenticity is always the child of today's inauthenticity. As Annie Chiu wisely said to me at Sun Luck Garden in Cleveland, Ohio: "If food is good, it's good. It doesn't matter if it's American, Chinese, Italian, even French. If it's good, it's good. Good food is good."

Index